*Proclaiming the*
# CHRISTMAS GOSPEL

# *Proclaiming the*
# CHRISTMAS GOSPEL

### ANCIENT SERMONS AND HYMNS FOR CONTEMPORARY CHRISTIAN INSPIRATION

*Edited by*

## John D. Witvliet *and* David Vroege

**BakerBooks**
Grand Rapids, Michigan

© 2004 by John D. Witvliet and David Vroege

Published by Baker Books
a division of Baker Publishing Group
P.O. Box 6287, Grand Rapids, MI 49516-6287
www.bakerbooks.com

Printed in the United States of America

Library of Congress Cataloging-in-Publication Data
Proclaiming the Christmas Gospel : ancient sermons and hymns for contemporary Christian inspiration / edited by John D. Witvliet and David Vroege.
          p.     cm.
    Includes bibliographical references.
    ISBN 0-8010-6405-8 (pbk.)
    1. Christmas sermons—Early works to 1800. I. Witvliet, John D.
II. Vroege, David, 1973–
BV4257.P76 2004
252'.615—dc22                                              2004013964

For permissions information, see Source Information and Bibliography at the back of the book.

# Contents

110150

# Preface

This volume was born out of an independent study course at Calvin Theological Seminary on historic sermons for key events in the Christian Year. An earlier course, "The Doctrine of Christ and the Services of the Christian Year," framed and motivated our study of sermons. We were looking to learn from the various ways in which Christian preachers have opened up the meaning of the events in Jesus' life to articulate their understanding of God and the Christian life. This is an important challenge for every preacher, whether or not they follow the liturgical year, given the biblical, theological, and pastoral significance of Jesus' birth, life, death, resurrection, ascension, and anticipated second coming. Our reading taught us a great deal, and also proved to be a source of encouragement and inspiration. We were particularly challenged by the sermons for Christmas that we discovered. Similar inspiration comes from the many ancient hymn texts that are still sung each Advent and Christmas season. We present these sermon and hymn texts both so that other students can easily replicate our study. We also sense that this collection could serve as an instructive set of supplemental readings for college, seminary, or congregational courses on church history, as well as for any Bible study group meeting near Christmas. Most of all, we present these texts so that all interested worshipers can find inspiration and instruction from listening to the Christmas gospel that has echoed through the church for two thousand years.

We are especially grateful to Professor David Rylaarsdam of Calvin Theological Seminary for assistance with the texts and translations of the sermons; to Joyce Borger for background research; to Rachel Klompmaker for assistance with the hymn texts; to Sue Rozeboom and Lisa Stracks for editorial assistance; to the Hekman Library at Calvin College and Calvin Theological Seminary for its excellent collection of resources; and to the faculty and administration of Calvin Theological Seminary for creating an environment that supports this kind of collaborative learning.

John D. Witvliet
Calvin Institute of Christian Worship,
Calvin College and Calvin Theological Seminary,
Grand Rapids, Michigan


David Vroege
All Nations Christian Reformed Church,
Halifax, Nova Scotia

# Introduction

Before you are the texts of thirteen Christmas sermons preached over a span of nearly eleven hundred years by some of the most noted preachers in the history of the Christian church. They are remarkably different sermons in length, tone, and purpose. What they share is a common concern to unpack the meaning of Christmas for congregations of Christian believers and seekers in memorable and pastorally significant ways.

Accompanying these sermons are hymn texts that compress the great themes and images of the Christmas gospel into lilting and memorable poetic lines. We have chosen texts that continue to be regularly sung in Christian worship to this day. Their current use is a sign that the historical distance between ancient and contemporary Christians can be spanned remarkably well in the context of meditation, prayer, and worship.

Our purposes in presenting this material are not primarily historical. While we present these texts in chronological order, this volume is not a balanced set of documents for a study of the history of preaching. It is not representative of all periods, locations, traditions, or even of the contribu-

tion of each individual preacher. Nor can this volume go
into details about various genres of preaching or modes of
preserving sermons. We hope that this work might moti-
vate further academic studies of these interesting topics.
But this collection is designed to provide raw materials for
any Christian worshiper to approach Christmas anew to
see again its life-giving message. These ancient texts are
presented for the purpose of inspiration, encouragement,
and ongoing learning.

## I. That We May Pray More Deeply

First, we hope this volume will evoke worship and prayer
as it invites readers to linger over the familiar narratives
and events of Christmas. These texts are not remarkable for
presenting anything new or innovative. Rather, they explore
the familiar territory of Matthew 1 and Luke 2, but in ways
that can help us appreciate more deeply the significance
of the Christmas gospel. Mindful of how difficult it was
to say anything new at Christmas, Augustine introduced
one Christmas sermon with these words: "Listen to what
you know, reflect on what you have heard, love what you
believe, and preach what you love. Just as we celebrate the
yearly coming of this day, so you may expect the sermon
that is this day's due."* Our prayer is that as you pause to
read these ancient texts, you, too, will reflect on what you
know and love what you believe.

We also hope that this little volume will stoke awareness that we stand in continuity with hosts of believers
across time and space. In a culture that values novelty and
innovation, what is remarkable about Christmas is that
it is the one time of year when worshipers who otherwise
prefer new music often want to sing old songs. In a culture

*Augustine, "On the Nativity," Selected Sermons of St. Augustine, ed. and trans.
Quincy Howe Jr., (Chicago: Holt, Rinehart and Winston, 1966), 49.

of emails and instant messages, the candles and carols of Christmas are for some worshipers the most tangible sign of continuity with the historic church that they will experience all year.

This longing for things of the past can easily slip into saccharine nostalgia, of course. But it is also quite a redeemable impulse, especially when it leads us to become aware of the enduring nature of the Christmas gospel and of God's faithfulness throughout the history of the church. For 2,000 years, in times of plenty and want, war and peace, health and sickness, these same narratives of Jesus' birth have, by the Spirit's power, evoked responses of wonder, love, and praise. Phillips Brooks' memorable phrase "The hopes and fears of all years are met in thee tonight" reminds us of the long procession of Christians who have found Jesus' birth to be a source of comfort and joy. Indeed, the texts in this book are a testimony to God's faithfulness.

It is especially significant that the majority of these texts come from the pre-Reformation church, from the millennium of church history that many American Protestants are either implicitly or explicitly taught to dismiss or ignore altogether. While some historians have not judged those centuries kindly, the preaching of the gospel was hardly stilled during these times, as even these few texts testify. Revisiting these centuries helps us not only gain a much more balanced awareness of the history of Christianity, but also helps us draw on rich resources that can inform our work in proclaiming and singing the gospel today.

In its commentary on the line "the communion of saints" in the Apostles' Creed, the Heidelberg Catechism explains that "believers one and all, as members of this community, share in Christ and in all his treasures and gifts." We hope that reading these texts is an experience of sharing in some of the treasure and gifts of the Christian tradition that will

11

prompt a deep sense of our continuity with the saints of
God who have gone before us.

## II. THAT WE MAY UNDERSTAND MORE
CLEARLY

Second, alert readers will find much to learn in the pages
of these sermons and hymns. There are many little theology
lessons tucked away in these texts. For one, these sermons
can help us sense how specific biblical narratives can open
up in so many different directions, depending on the goal
and theological lens that we bring to the text. Nearly every
sermon here is based on the nativity narratives of Luke 2
and/or Matthew 1–2. Yet each sermon explores them in
different ways, dwelling on different complementary theological themes.

Some sermons dwell on the mystery of Christ's incarnation, framing the nativity narratives through the lens of
John 1. Augustine, for example, announces that "his divine
power was confined in the body of an infant without being
withdrawn from the whole mass of the universe." Here
the attention is focused on the mystery of God becoming
flesh.

Other sermons probe the nature of divine atonement, the
way in which Jesus' life, death, and resurrection accomplish
salvation—especially sermons that quote Romans more than
John. Leo, for example, preaches, "Omnipotent Lord engages this extremely savage enemy, not in his own majesty
but in our lowliness, bringing against him the very same
form and the very same nature that had been overcome,
indeed sharing in our mortality but wholly without sin."
Here the attention is on the conquest of evil or the plan for
divine redemption.

Still other sermons explore the mystery of our union with
Christ. John Calvin, for example, concludes his sermon with

a beautiful invitation to the Lord's Supper: "Let us not stop drawing near to our Lord Jesus Christ and being assured that it is he in whom we will find all good, all rejoicing, and all glory, although it seems that he is still, as it were, in the stable and in the manger, wrapped with swaddling clothes." Here the attention is focused on our sharing in Christ and all Christ's benefits.

Indeed, Christmas, like Easter and Pentecost, connects with each major loci or theme of traditional systematic theology. It is possible to imagine Christmas sermons that could explore the doctrines of Trinity, creation, providence, redemption, and eschatology. A single event in Christ's life, such as his birth, is a prism that focuses and opens up the whole spectrum of themes that comprise Christian teaching. It is an instructive theological exercise to name exactly how this is so (and one can imagine this being a wonderful exam question for courses in theology!).

These sermons also teach us by occasionally overstepping their bounds. Not infrequently, these sermons fall into over-interpretation of the narrative details of the text. It was a common feature of patristic and medieval Scripture interpretation to read significance in every detail of the biblical story, at times in imaginative, even fanciful ways—a practice that continues in many contemporary Christmas celebrations. Our minds, like the minds of the ancients, frequently fill in narrative details and attach meanings to them that may tell us more about our own situation than what the text actually says! This collection of texts is relatively innocent compared with other texts we might have chosen. Still, readers may occasionally wonder if a small detail in the texts gets more attention than it deserves.

More ominously, these texts can help us see how much of biblical interpretation actually turns out to be imposed on the text from the outside. Most problematic are strands of anti-Semitism that mark the history of Christian preaching. When unpacking Gospel narratives, Christian preachers have been frequently tempted to assign blame to a particular group of a people (the Jews), rather than to a group that elicits similar behavior as those found in the text (such as those who refuse the gospel message). These texts from the tradition come to us with warning and caution.

## III. THAT WE MAY PREACH MORE TRULY

Finally, these sermons, historically distant though they are, can also inform and challenge contemporary preaching. True, reading texts from centuries ago does not yield illustrations of contemporary cultural life or rhetorical strategies for engaging postmodern congregations. Further, these sermons represent very different ideas of what a sermon should be like. But there are many things such a collection can do in unique ways, especially because of the historical distance between us and the texts.

First, studying these sermons reminds us of the multiple theological lenses and homiletic aims that we can use to unpack these nativity narratives. Many preachers unwittingly put the same doctrinal frame around many—if not most or all—narrative texts: no matter where a sermon starts, it always opens up through a particular doctrine. Some preach every Christian festival sermon from an atonement-focused theology. Other preachers turn most sermons into treatises on Christian obedience or explorations of eschatological hope. However, Christians need a balanced diet of theological themes and images. Thus, one helpful discipline for any preacher is self-awareness and intentionality about preaching not only a balanced diet of texts, but also a balanced diet of theological themes.

Similar balance is helpful when thinking about the aims of preaching. The aim of a sermon might be stirring true worship, teaching new believers, converting unbelievers, or prodding worshipers to faithful Christian living. Arguably, one underrepresented genre in our own time is doxological preaching, preaching that prompts worship (e.g. "so then let us stand in awe and wonder at this mystery of faith"), a mode that is amply represented here. Given the hurried celebrations and surface-level emotions that mark some contemporary cultural celebrations of Christmas, perhaps we need more of this doxological preaching. One mark of a good Christmas sermon might simply be its ability to prepare a congregation to sing "Silent Night" in a spirit of contrite and quiet awe.

Second, any sermon from times or cultures different than our own can teach us to be alert to the rhetoric of preaching. Every culture and language has a different sense of how long a good sentence should be and what figures of speech are most appropriate. These differences can make us more aware of our own rhetorical tendencies. While generalizations about all thirteen sermons here are difficult to make, it is interesting to speculate how many entries these few sermons would be able to generate for an imaginary new edition of Bartlett's Christian Quotations. Many of them feature several pithy aphorisms that pack a memorable rhetorical punch. Several of these quotations are highlighted in the text and may well find their way into contemporary sermons, church bulletins, and email signatures.

Further, note how these sermons are permeated with the language of Scripture. Most of these sermons were preached long before preachers were able to hold Bibles in their hands, flipping back and forth from one text to another, yet they are infused by scriptural language. As Augustine advised, in his famous treatise "On Christian Doctrine":

> It is especially necessary for the man who is bound to speak wisely, even though he cannot speak eloquently, to retain in memory the words of Scripture. For the more he discerns the poverty in his own speech, the more he ought to draw on the riches of the Scripture, so that what he says in his own

words he may prove by the words of Scripture and so that
he himself, though small and weak in his own discourse,
may gain strength and power from the confirming testimony
of great men.*

Most of the preachers represented in this volume had
large portions of Scripture committed to memory, and their
language reflects it. True, scriptural language does not make
a sermon scriptural; at times the use of a particular image
or phrase is forced at best. But often phrases and imagery
drawn from various parts of the Bible come together in
these sermons to generate apt and evocative passages, living
examples of the maxim "Scripture interprets Scripture."

Third, these sermons also provide interesting case studies
for thinking about preaching on events in Jesus' life. Every
year, most preachers are asked to preach memorably on
each key event in Jesus' life. What marks good preaching at
these times? In our own studies, we have returned to several
basic questions or criteria when thinking about sermons for
festivals of the Christian Year:

1. Does the sermon tell the story and orient us to a
   particular biblical narrative?
2. Does the sermon put the specific story in a larger
   context as a window into the whole gospel? That is,
   does the sermon orient us in salvation history? Does it
   challenge us to re-imagine our past and our future?
3. Does the sermon open up the meaning of the historical event for our understanding of God and God's
   economy of salvation? (That is, does it attend to something *more* than history?)
4. Does the sermon open up the meaning of the event
   to instruct our living of the Christian life?

---

*Augustine, "On Christian Doctrine," in *A Select Library of the Nicene and Post-Nicene Fathers of the Christian Church*, ed. Philip Schaff, 1st ser. (Grand Rapids: Eerdmans, n.d.), 4.5.8.

5. Does the sermon consciously situate itself in the context of the liturgy or the worship service in which it is set? Does it prompt the authentic worship of all God's people?

Indeed, the best sermons for the Christian Year feature sustained attention to original biblical narrative, disciplined imagination in opening up those narratives for what they say about God, and pastoral, accessible ways of connecting that message with the lives of worshipers. For students of preaching, the following sermons present interesting examples for working out these dimensions of Christian Year preaching. We hope that offering them will prompt new and fresh thinking about how to preach the Christmas gospel faithfully and effectively.

# O GLADSOME LIGHT

A third-century Greek hymn for evening prayer, this English text is based on a translation by Robert Seymour Bridges (1899).

*O gladsome light, O grace*
*Of our Creator's face,*
*The eternal splendor wearing:*
*Celestial, holy, blest,*
*Our Savior Jesus Christ,*
*Joyful in your appearing.*

*As fades the day's last light,*
*We see the lamps of night*
*Our common hymn outpouring;*
*O God of might unknown,*
*You, the incarnate Son,*
*And Spirit blest adoring.*

*To you of right belongs*
*All praise of holy songs,*
*O Son of God, Life-giver;*
*You, therefore, O Most High,*
*The world does glorify*
*And shall exalt forever.*

~ SERMON ~

# 1

# Jerome,
## A.D. 340–420

*O*ur collection begins with the work of one of the
most thorough students of the Bible in the early
church, and with a sermon that may well have
been preached in Bethlehem itself, in a church built to
honor Jesus' birth (the Basilica of the Nativity). Jerome
was a pioneer biblical scholar, who translated the entire
Hebrew Old Testament and the Greek New Testament
into Latin, and is known for his work in assessing the
validity of biblical manuscripts. After living in Rome,
Antioch, and Constantinople, he worked for almost thirty-
five years in Bethlehem.

Most of Jerome's Christmas sermon consists of phrase-
by-phrase commentary on Luke 2. Jerome's pastoral
intent can be seen in his advice to the poor to take
comfort in Jesus' lowly birth. He takes time to ponder
each textual detail, often citing other Scripture texts that
provide insight on the meaning of a given phrase—though

*occasionally Jerome makes more of each detail than the text warrants (did Joseph really not touch baby Jesus?). The sermon also includes a short treatise on why Jesus' birth should be celebrated on Christmas (in light of a calendar dispute with other Christians of the time) and culminates with a summons to Christmas praise. In a move emulated by preachers of every generation, Jerome ends with an apology for preaching too long ("We have forgotten our resolution and said more than we intended"!).*

---

"She laid him in a manger, because there was no room for them in the inn." (Luke 2:7) His mother laid him in a manger. Joseph did not dare to touch him, for he knew he had not been begotten of him. In awe, he rejoiced at a son, but he did not dare to touch the Son.

"She laid him in a manger." Why in a manger? That the prophecy of Isaiah, the prophet, might be fulfilled: "An ox knows its owner, and a donkey, its master's manger." (Isa. 1:3) In another place, it is written: "You save both humans and animals, O LORD." (Ps. 36:6) If you are human, eat the Bread; if you are an animal, come to the manger.

"Because there was no room for them in the inn." Appropriately said: "There was no room for them in the inn," for Jewish unbelief had overflowed into everything. He found no room in the Holy of Holies that shone with gold, precious stones, pure silk, and silver. He is born in the midst of gold and riches, but in the midst of dung, in a stable (wherever there is a stable, there is also dung) where our sins were more filthy than the dung. He is born on a dunghill in order to lift up those who come from it; "from a dunghill he lifts up the poor." (Ps. 113:7) He is born on a dunghill, where Job, too, sat and afterwards was crowned.

"There was no room for them in the inn." The poor should take great comfort from this. Joseph and Mary, the mother of the Lord, had no servant boy, no maid servant. From Nazareth in Galilee, they come all alone; they own no work animals; they are their own masters and servants. Here is a new thought. They go to the wayside inn, not into the city, for poverty is too timid to venture among the rich. Note the extent of their poverty. They go to a wayside inn. Holy Scripture did not say that the inn was on the road, but on a wayside off the road, not on it, but beyond it; not on the way of the Law, but on the byway of the Gospel,

*O, if only I were permitted to see that manger in which the Lord lay! Now, as an honor to Christ, we have taken away the manger of clay and have replaced it with crib of silver, but more precious to me is the one that has been removed.*

on the byroad. There was no other place unoccupied for the birth of the Savior except a manger, a manger to which were tethered cattle and donkeys. O, if only I were permitted to see that manger in which the Lord lay! Now, as an honor to Christ, we have taken away the manger of clay and have replaced it with crib of silver, but more precious to me is the one that has been removed. Silver and gold are appropriate for unbelievers; Christian faith is worthy of the manger that is made of clay. He who was born in that manger cared nothing for gold and silver. I do not find fault with those who made the change in the cause of honor (nor do I look with disfavor upon those in the Temple who made vessels of gold), but I marvel at the Lord, the Creator of the universe, who is born, not surrounded by gold and silver, but by mud and clay.

"There were shepherds in the fields nearby keeping watch." (Luke 2:8) They will not find Christ unless they keep watch, which is the shepherd's duty. Christ is not found except by the alert. That is why the bride says: "I was sleeping, but my heart was awake." (Song 5:2) "Indeed the guardian of Israel neither slumbers nor sleeps." (Ps. 121:4) There were shepherds in the fields nearby. Herod was there; the high

*I marvel at the Lord, the Creator of the universe, who is born, not surrounded by gold and silver, but by mud and clay.*

priests, the Pharisees were there; while they were sleeping, Christ is found in a lonely grotto.

"Shepherds keeping watch over their flock at night." They were guarding their flock so that the wolf would not attack while they slept. They were keeping careful watch; the threat to the flock from the treachery of wild animals was reason enough. They were keeping watch, as it were, over the Lord's flock, but they could not keep it safe; therefore they urgently asked the Lord to come and save it.

"An angel of the Lord stood by them." (Luke 2:9) They who were so alert deserved to have an angel come to them.

"The glory of God shone around them, and they were terrified." Human fear is unable to gaze on a magnificent and majestic vision. Because they were so thoroughly terrified, the angel speaks and, like a healing salve applied to wounds, restores their confidence.

"Do not be afraid," for you cannot grasp what I am saying if you are paralyzed by fear.

"There has been born to you today in the town of David a Savior, who is Christ the Lord." (Luke 2:11) These are weighty words. While they were so astonished, "suddenly there was with the angel a multitude of the heavenly host praising God and saying." (Luke 2:13) Since one angel had announced the nativity of the Lord, and so that it would not seem that only one testifies, the entire host resounds in one song of praise: "Glory to God in the highest, and peace on earth among those of good will." (Luke 2:14) If sins, according to the heretics, are a daily occurrence in heaven, how can there be glory in heaven, and why is peace prayed for on earth? Notice what the Gospel says. In heaven, where there is no conflict, glory rules; on earth, where every day is warfare, peace prevails. On earth peace. Peace among whom? Among humans. Why are the Gentiles without peace; why, too, the Jews? That is exactly the reason for the qualification: peace among those of good will, among those who acknowledge the birth of Christ.

"The shepherds said to one another, 'Let us go to Bethlehem.'" (Luke 2:15) Let us leave the deserted Temple and go to Bethlehem. "And see the word which was made." Truly alert, they did not say, "Let us see the child, let us find out what is being announced"; but, "Let us see the word that has been made."

"In the beginning was the Word. . . . And the Word was made flesh." (John 1:1, 14) The Word that has always been, let us see how it was made for us. "And see this word which was made, which the Lord has made, and has made known to us." (cf. Luke 2:15) This same Word made itself, inasmuch as this same Word is the Lord. Let us see, therefore, in what way this same Word, the Lord himself, has made himself and has made his flesh known to us. Because we could not see him as long as he was the Word, let us see his flesh because it is flesh; let us see how the Word was made flesh.

"So they went with haste." (Luke 2:16) The eager longing of their souls gave wings to their feet; they could not keep pace with their desire to see him: "So they went with haste." Because they ran so eagerly, they find him whom they were seeking. Let us see what they find.

"Mary and Joseph." If she were truly the wife, it would be improper to say, they found the wife and the husband; but the Gospel named the woman first, then the man. What does Holy Scripture say? "They found Mary and Joseph": they found Mary, the mother, and Joseph, the guardian.

"And the babe lying in the manger." And when they had seen him, they understood concerning the word, what had been told them concerning this child.

"But Mary kept in mind all these words, pondering them in her heart." (cf. Luke 2:16–19) What does pondering mean? It must have meant weighing carefully in her heart, meditating within herself, and comparing notes in her heart. A certain interpreter explains "pondering in her heart" as follows: she was a holy woman, had read the Sacred Scriptures, knew the prophets, and was recalling that the angel Gabriel had said to her the same things that the prophets had foretold. She was pondering in her heart whether the prophets anticipated the words: "The Holy Spirit will come upon you

*Since she was pondering in her heart,*
*let us, likewise, meditate in our hearts*
*that on this day Christ is born.*

and the power of the Most High will overshadow you; and therefore the Holy One to be born will be called the Son of God." (Luke 1:35) Gabriel had said that; Isaiah had foretold: "The virgin will be with child and will give birth to a son." (Isa. 7:14) She had read the latter; she had heard the former. She looked at the child lying before her; she saw the child crying in the manger; she saw there the Son of God, her Son, her one and only Son; she looked at him, and in her musing, she compared what she had heard with what she had read and with what she herself perceived.

Since she was pondering in her heart, let us, likewise, meditate in our hearts that on this day Christ is born. There are some who think that he was born on Epiphany. We do not condemn the opinion of others, but follow the conclusions of our own study. "Let everyone be convinced in his own mind and perhaps the Lord will make it clear to each one." (cf. Rom. 14:5; Phil. 3:15) Both those who say the Lord is born then, and we who say he is born today, worship one Lord, acknowledge one Babe. Let us review a few facts, however, not to rebuke others by our reasoning, but to confirm our own position. We are not airing our own opinion, but supporting tradition. The common consent of the world is contrary to the thinking of this province. Perhaps someone may object: "Christ was born here; are they who are far away better informed than those who are close by? Who told you?" They who are of this province, of course, the apostles, Peter and Paul, and the rest of them. You have rejected tradition; we have accepted it; Peter who was here with John, who lived here with James, taught us also in the West. The apostles are both your teachers and ours.

Here is another fact. The Jews, at that time, were ruling in Judea. Furthermore, the Acts of the Apostles reports: "On that day a great persecution broke out and those who believed were scattered abroad." (Acts 8:1) They went into Cyprus and into Antioch, and the dispersed Jews penetrated the whole world. Since, therefore, the Jews were in power for forty-two years after the Ascension of the Lord, everywhere else there was peace; here, alone, there was war. Tradition could, then, be preserved more easily in the West than in Judea where there was conflict. After forty-two years, the armies of Vespasian and Titus arrived; Jerusalem was overthrown and destroyed; all the Jews and Christians were driven out, every one of them. Until the time of Hadrian, Jerusalem remained a wilderness; there was not one Jew nor one Christian left in this entire province. Then Hadrian came and, because another revolution of the Jews broke out in Galilee, he destroyed what had remained of the city. He further proclaimed by law that no Jew was permitted to approach Jerusalem, and brought new settlers into the city from different provinces. I might mention that Hadrian's name was Aelius Hadrian, and that, after he destroyed Jerusalem, he called the restored city Aelia.

Why am I saying all this? Because they say to us: This is where the apostles lived; this is where the tradition has been established. Now, we say that Christ was born today; on Epiphany, he was reborn. You who maintain he was born on Epiphany prove for us generation and regeneration. When did he receive baptism, unless you face the consequence that on the same day he was born and reborn? Even nature is in agreement with our claim, for the world itself bears witness to our statement. Up to this day, darkness increases; from this day on, it decreases; light increases, darkness decreases; the day waxes, error wanes; truth advances. For us today, the Sun of Justice is born. In conclusion, consider another point. Between the Lord and John the Baptist, there are

*Because pride never brings salvation,*
*but humility does.*

six months. If you study the nativity of John in relation to Christ's, you will see that they are six months apart.

Since we have touched on many things and have heard the Babe crying in the manger and have adored him there, let us continue our adoration of him today. Let us pick him up in our arms and adore him as the Son of God. Mighty God who for so long a time thundered in heaven and did not redeem humanity, cries and as a babe redeems him. Why do I say all this? Because pride never brings salvation, but humility does. As long as the Son of God was in heaven, he was not adored; he descends to earth and is adored. He had beneath him the sun, the moon, the angels, and he was not adored; on earth, he is born perfect man, a whole man, to heal the whole world. Whatever of human nature he did not assume, he could not save; if he assumed only the body and not the soul, he did not save the soul. Did he, then, save what is of less value and not redeem that which is of greater? If, however, they admit that he saved the soul that he assumed, then consider that, just as the soul is superior to the body, reason is similarly the ruling faculty of the soul itself. If Christ did not redeem human rationality, neither did he save the soul which is less. You reply that he did not take upon himself a human mind, in order that his heart might be free from human vices, evil thoughts, and desires. Do you mean, therefore, that if he could not control what he made, I should consider myself unworthy if I cannot conquer what he should have conquered?

We have forgotten our resolution and said more than we intended; the mind planned to do one thing, the tongue in its zeal slipped ahead. Let us be ready now to give our attention to the Bishop and earnestly take to heart what he has to say on what I have left out. Let us bless the Lord, to whom be glory forever and ever. Amen.

# SAVIOR OF THE NATIONS, COME

A fourth-century text by Ambrose of Milan, translated into German by Martin Luther and into English by Calvin Seerveld.

*Savior of the nations, come,*
*Show yourself, the virgin's son.*
*Fill with wonder, all the earth,*
*That our God chose such a birth.*

*Not by human power or seed*
*Did the woman's womb conceive;*
*Only by the Spirit's breath*
*Was the Word of God made flesh.*

*Mary then was found with child,*
*Still a virgin, chaste and mild.*
*God had favored her with grace*
*To receive the Prince of Peace.*

*Christ laid down his majesty,*
*Passed through dark Gethsemane.*
*Though he left his Father's home,*
*Christ now sits on God's own throne.*

*Since the star at Bethlehem*
*Brought new light to earth again,*
*May our faith shine bright each day;*
*Faithful God, keep sin away.*

*Christ in glory, intercede*
*For your creatures' suffering need.*
*Let your resurrecting power*
*Soon complete the victory hour.*

*Praise to you, O Lord, we sing.*
*Praise to Christ, our newborn King!*
*With the Father, Spirit, one,*
*Let your lasting kingdom come.*

# 2

## Augustine of Hippo,
### 354–430

*ne of the most influential leaders of the early
church, Augustine was already a celebrated preacher
in his own day. Despite his popularity and skill,
Augustine did not preach to Rome's cultural elite in
its heyday, but rather to common Christians in the North
African city of Hippo, located in what is now Algeria.*

*This brief sermon is a short meditation on the mystery
of the incarnation, the wonders of God becoming
human. It was preached in the year 396, nine years after
Augustine's baptism by Ambrose and in only the second
year of his thirty-five-year tenure as bishop. Originally
preached in Latin, the text gives hints of the masterful use
of rhetorical devices, such as alliteration, paradox, and
rhetorical questions, that were especially prominent early
in his preaching career. Augustine's goal in this sermon is*

*to invite the faithful to offer praise to God and to rejoice at the wonder of Christ's coming.*

⤙ ⤚

The birthday of our Lord and Savior Jesus Christ, the day on which "Truth sprang from the earth" (Ps. 85:11) and Day from Day was born into our day, this day which has dawned once more, brought round again by the cycle of the year to be celebrated by us. "Let us rejoice and make merry on it." (Ps. 118:24) All that springs from the humility of this sublime moment is grasped by the faith of Christians, while far from the comprehension of the godless; since God "has hidden these things from the wise and the prudent, and revealed them to the little ones." (Luke 10:21)

So let the humble hold fast to the humility of God, so that this wonderful support may, like a beast of burden, lighten the burden of their weakness, and they may arrive at the heights of God. As for the wise and the prudent, they aim at the loftiness of God without believing in his humble lowliness; and so, by overstepping his humility and not reaching his loftiness, they have remained, empty and weightless, inflated and elated, dangling, as it were, at a windy middle level between heaven and earth.

They are indeed wise and prudent, but in the affairs of this world, not of the one by whom the world was made. Because if they were possessed of the true wisdom, which is from God and is God, they would understand that it was possible for flesh to be taken on by God without his being changed into flesh; they would understand that he took to himself what he was not, while remaining what he was; and that he came to us in a man without ever departing from the Father; and that he continued to be what he is, while appearing to us as what we are; and that his divine power was confined in the body of an infant without being withdrawn from the whole mass of the universe.

The whole universe is his work as he remains with the Father; his work as he comes to us is the virgin's child-bearing. The virgin mother indeed provided a demonstration of his greatness, being found a virgin after giving birth just as she was a virgin before conceiving; being found with child by

*. . . he took to himself what he was not,*
*while remaining what he was; . . . he continued*
*to be what he is, while appearing to us*
*as what we are . . .*

her husband, she did not conceive by him; she carried a man not conceived by man; all the more blessed and admirable for receiving the gift of fertility without losing that of integrity. They prefer to regard this stupendous miracle as fiction rather than fact. Thus in Christ, true God and true man, they despise the human because they cannot believe it; they do not believe the divine because they cannot despise

*Christ has been born, a man; he has been born*
*of a woman; and each sex has been honored.*

it. We, however, find the body of man in the humility of God all the more welcome, the more contemptible it seems to them; and the more they think it is impossible, the more divine it seems to us that a man was born by a virgin bringing him forth.

So then, let us celebrate the birthday of the Lord with all due festive gatherings. Let men rejoice, let women rejoice. Christ has been born, a man; he has been born of a woman; and each sex has been honored. Now therefore, let everyone, having been condemned in the first man, pass over to the second. It was a woman who sold us death; a woman who bore us life. "The likeness of the flesh of sin" (Rom. 8:3) has been born, so that the flesh of sin might be cleansed and

31

purified. And thus it is not the flesh that is to be faulted, but the fault that must die in order that the nature may live; because one has been born without fault, in whom the other who was at fault may be reborn.

Rejoice, holy brothers, who, choosing above all to follow Christ, have not sought to get married. The one you have found to be so worth following did not come to you by way of marriage, in order to enable you to set aside that by which you came into the world. For you came by way of carnal marriage, without which he came to his spiritual marriage; and he has given you the grace to turn your backs on any thought of weddings, because it is you above all whom he has invited to the wedding. The reason you have not sought the state from which you were born is that you have loved more than others the one who was not so born. Rejoice, holy sisters, virgins; for you a virgin gave birth to the one whom you may marry without loss of virginity; neither by conceiving nor by giving birth can you lose what you love.

"Rejoice, you just;" (Ps. 33:1) it is the birthday of the Justifier.

Rejoice, you who are weak and sick; it is the birthday of the Savior, the Healer.

Rejoice, captives; it is the birthday of the Redeemer.

Rejoice, slaves; it is the birthday of the one who makes you lords.

Rejoice, free people; it is the birthday of the one who makes you free.

Rejoice, all Christians; it is the birthday of Christ.

Born of his mother, he commended this day to the ages, while born of his Father he created all ages. That birth could have no mother, while this one required no man as father. To sum up, Christ was born both of a Father and of a mother; both without a father and without a mother; of

32

a Father as God, of a mother as man; without a mother as God, without a father as man. Therefore, "who will recount his begetting," (Isa. 53:8) whether that one without time or this

> *The one who holds the world in being was lying in a manger; he was simultaneously speechless infant and Word. The heavens cannot contain him, a woman carried him in her bosom.*

one without seed; that one without beginning or this one without precedent; that one which never was not, or this one which never was before or after; that one which has no end, or this one which has its beginning in its end?

Rightly therefore did the prophets foretell that he would be born, while the heavens and the angels announced that he had been. The one who holds the world in being was lying in a manger; he was simultaneously speechless infant and Word. The heavens cannot contain him, a woman carried him in her bosom. She was ruling our ruler, carrying the one in whom we are, suckling our bread. O manifest infirmity and wondrous humility in which was thus concealed total divinity! Omnipotence was ruling the mother on whom infancy was depending; was nourishing on truth

> *O manifest infirmity and wondrous humility in which was thus concealed total divinity!*

the mother whose breasts it was sucking. May he bring his gifts to perfection in us, since he did not shrink from making his own our tiny beginnings; and may he make us into children of God, since for our sake he was willing to be made a child of man.

# LET ALL MORTAL FLESH KEEP SILENCE

From the liturgy of St. James, as celebrated in Jerusalem, possibly as early as the late fourth century, this English text is based on a translation by Gerard Moultrie (1864).

> *Let all mortal flesh keep silence,*
> *And with fear and trembling stand;*
> *Set your minds on things eternal,*
> *For with blessing in his hand*
> *Christ our Lord to earth descended,*
> *Came our homage to command.*
>
> *King of kings, yet born of Mary,*
> *Once upon the earth he stood;*
> *Lord of lords we now perceive him*
> *In the body and the blood.*
> *He has given to all the faithful*
> *His own self for heavenly food.*
>
> *Rank on rank the host of heaven*
> *Stream before him on the way,*
> *As the Light of Light, descending*
> *From the realms of endless day,*
> *Comes, the powers of hell to vanquish,*
> *Clears the gloom of hell away.*
>
> *At his feet the six-winged seraph,*
> *Cherubim with sleepless eye*
> *Veil their faces to his presence,*
> *As with ceaseless voice they cry:*
> *"Alleluia, alleluia!*
> *Alleluia, Lord Most High!"*

# 3

## Leo the Great,
### ca. 400—461

*eo was an influential pope in the closing years of the patristic age. He functioned not only as a leader of the church but also of society, working to protect Rome from barbarian attacks. He preached in Rome only on the "solemnities," the great feast days of the Christian year, including Christmas. His sermons are both compact and solemn. His Christmas sermons focus not on the nativity narratives of Luke 2, but rather the theological significance of Jesus' birth in light of the whole scope of New Testament teaching. Leo's sermons are designed to be more like creeds than Scripture commentaries.*

*Though preached in the year 440, Leo begins his sermon by saying that Jesus was born "this day." This practice of imagining that worship brings us back in time echoes the practice of Jewish Passover celebrations. At Passover, participants recounted, "In every generation each one of us should regard himself as though he himself had gone forth from Egypt." Likewise, in Exodus 13:8, Moses commanded, "On that day, tell your son, 'I do this because of what the Lord did for me when I came out of Egypt.' " For generations after the exodus, the people were to celebrate Passover as if they had been there, a kind of liturgical "time warp." Even today, we experience this time warp every time we sing "Yea, Lord, we greet you, born this happy morning."*

Our Savior, dearly beloved, was born this day. Let us rejoice. No, there cannot rightly be any room for sorrow in a place where life has been born. By casting out fear of death, life fills us with joy about the promised eternity. No one has been cut off from a share in this excitement. All share together a single reason for joy. Our Lord, finding no one free of guilt, has come to liberate all.

Let saints exult, for victory lies within their reach.
Let sinners rejoice, for they have been called to forgiveness.
Let heathens take heart, for they have been summoned to life.

God's Son, in the "fullness of time," (Gal. 4:4; Eph. 1:10) which the "inscrutable depths of divine wisdom" had ordained, (Wis. 2:24) took on human nature to reconcile it to its Maker. In that way, the devil who invented death (Wis. 2:24) might be overcome through that very thing which he had overcome. In the conflict undertaken on our behalf, battle was joined on the most remarkably fair terms. Omnipotent Lord engages this extremely savage enemy, not in his own majesty but in our lowliness, bringing against

36

him the very same form and the very same nature that had been overcome, indeed sharing in our mortality but wholly without sin. What is read about birth in general

> *. . . the devil who invented death might be overcome through that very thing which he had overcome.*

does not apply to this one: "No one is clean from stain, not even an infant, had his life on earth lasted only a single day." (Job 14:4–5)

Into this unique birth, then, nothing has passed over from the lustful passion of the flesh, nothing flowed from the law of sin. Chosen is a royal virgin from the shoot of David. Destined to become pregnant with the sacred fruit, she conceives an offspring (both divine and human) in her spirit—before she does so in her body. So that she might not, in being uninformed about the divine plan, become frightened by its unusual effects, she learns from conversation with an angel what work was to be accomplished in her by the Holy Spirit.

She did not believe that her honor would be compromised, she who would soon be the mother of God. Why indeed would she have any misgivings about the conception on account of its unusual nature? She has been promised its accomplishment through the power of the Most High. Her confidence rested on a faith reinforced by the testimony of a miracle that had come as a precursor. Elizabeth has been given an unhoped-for fruitfulness. For the one who had given conception to a sterile woman could undoubtedly give it to a virgin as well.

Consequently, the Word of God, God the Son of God, who "in the beginning was with God, through whom all things were made and without whom nothing was made," (John 1:1–3) was himself made human in order to free human

37

beings from eternal death. He adapted himself to take up our lowliness without diminishing his majesty. Remaining what he was and taking on what he was not, he united the true "form of a servant" with the form in which he is equal to God the Father. (Phil. 2:6–7) He grafted together both natures in such a union that glorification should not overwhelm the lower nor humbling diminish the higher.

When, therefore, the identity of each substance is preserved and they join in a single person, majesty takes up humility, strength takes up weakness, eternity takes up

*He grafted together both natures in such a*
*union that glorification should not overwhelm*
*the lower nor humbling diminish the higher.*

mortality. To pay the debt of our condition, his invincible nature pours forth into a vulnerable one. True God and true man are combined into the unity of the Lord. So, as suited our healing, one and the same "Mediator between God and human beings" (1 Tim. 2:5) was able both to die (because of his humanity) and to rise again (because of his divinity). Appropriately, this birth of salvation brought absolutely no corruption to the virgin's integrity, for giving birth to truth served to guard her honor.

Such, then, dearly beloved, was the Nativity appropriate for Christ, "the power of God and the wisdom of God."

*. . . majesty takes up humility, strength takes*
*up weakness, eternity takes up mortality.*

(1 Cor. 1:24) By it he both conforms to us through humanity and rises above us through divinity. Were he not indeed true God, he could apply no remedy. Were he not indeed true man, he could show no example. Exulting angels sing at the Lord's

Birth, "Glory to God in the highest," and proclaim, "On earth, peace to people of good will." (Luke 2:14) They indeed see the heavenly Jerusalem being constructed from all the nations of the world. How much should the lowliness of

> *Were he not indeed true God, he could apply no remedy. Were he not indeed true man, he could show no example.*

human beings rejoice over this indescribable work of divine pity when the loftiness of angels so delights in it?

As a result, dearly beloved, let us give "thanks to God the Father" (Col. 1:12) through his Son, in the Holy Spirit. "Because of that great love of his with which he loved us," he took pity on us, and, "when we were dead through our sins, he brought us to life through Christ," (Eph. 2:4–5) so that we might be a "new creature" (2 Cor. 5:17; Gal. 6:15) in him, a new handiwork.

Let us therefore put aside the old human being along with its actions." (Col. 3:8–9) Since we have become sharers in

> *Realize, O Christian, your dignity.*

the Birth of Christ, let us renounce "works of the flesh." (Gal. 5:19)

Realize, O Christian, your dignity. Once made a "participant in the divine nature," (2 Peter 1:4) do not return to your former detestable character by a life unworthy of that dignity.

Remember whose head it is and whose body of which you constitute a member. (1 Cor. 6:14)

Recall how you had been jerked "from the power of darkness and brought into the light and the kingdom" of

God. (Col. 1:13) Through the Sacrament of Baptism you were made "temple of the Holy Spirit." (1 Cor. 6:19)

Do not drive away such a dweller by your wicked actions and subject yourself again to slavery under the devil, because your price (1 Cor. 6:20, 7:23) is the very blood of Christ, because he "will judge" you "in truth" (Ps. 95:13) who has redeemed you in mercy, Christ our Lord. Amen.

# OF THE FATHER'S LOVE BEGOTTEN

Based on a Latin poem by Marcus Aurelius Prudentius, from a collection of devotional poetry from 405, published in what is now Spain. This English text is based on a translation by John Mason Neale (1854) and Henry W. Baker (1859).

*Of the Father's love begotten*
*Ere the worlds began to be,*
*He is Alpha and Omega—*
*He the source, the ending he,*
*Of the things that are, that have been,*
*And that future years shall see*
*Evermore and evermore.*

*O that birth forever blessed,*
*When a virgin, blest with grace,*
*By the Holy Ghost conceiving,*
*Bore the Savior of our race;*
*And the babe, the world's Redeemer,*
*First revealed his sacred face,*
*Evermore and evermore.*

*This is he whom seers in old time*
*Chanted of with one accord,*
*Whom the voices of the prophets*
*Promised in their faithful word;*
*Now he shines, the long-expected;*
*Let creation praise its Lord*
*Evermore and evermore.*

*Let the heights of heaven adore him;*
*Angel hosts, his praises sing:*
*Powers, dominions, bow before him*
*And extol our God and King;*
*Let no tongue on earth be silent,*
*Every voice in concert ring*
*Evermore and evermore.*

*Christ, to you, with God the Father*
*And the Spirit, there shall be*
*Hymn and chant and high thanksgiving*
*And the shout of jubilee:*
*Honor, glory, and dominion*
*And eternal victory*
*Evermore and evermore!*
*Amen.*

# 4

## Caesarius of Arles,
### 470–543

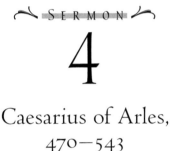aesarius was bishop of Arles (in what is now southeastern France). He was a careful student of earlier Latin theology, especially that of Augustine, and an ardent defender of Christian orthodoxy. He was a strong supporter of popular preaching, and worked to establish preaching as a regular duty not only for bishops, but also for priests. He encouraged priests who had minimal training to simply preach the sermons of others, including his, and he helped to disseminate collections of sermons for this purpose.

Upon first reading, this seems like an Easter sermon. Caesarius even admits it: "The extent of the divine mercy has taken me quite far away from the present feast." The goal here is purely pastoral. Caesarius used every occasion to explain the basic substance of the gospel, especially mindful of a congregation that included people with little exposure to the Christian faith.

On this day, dear brothers and sisters, Christ was born to us. Let us prepare for him in our hearts a dwelling full of obedient service. Let us prepare a crib, a cradle brilliant with the flowers of a good life and the perpetual sweetness of its fragrance. Let us receive the tiny little Lord in our hearts. May he grow and make progress there, nourished by faith; may he ascend to youth there on the steps of life; and may he exercise the powers which are mentioned in the gospel.

Within us the Lord has a blind person to whom he can give light, a lame person whose step he can restore and bring to the path of truth without stumbling. In this room he finds a dead person, a corpse stretched out. He even finds a stinking cadaver which the kindly one who raises from the dead may bring back from the tomb of sin. What the Lord did in those who were dead he does in the living. He raises a person to life in the room of the heart, just as he did the daughter of the head of the synagogue, provided that the person repents of sins of deadly thoughts. Since a person who, with evil intent, has decided to sin is already dead, the Lord raises that person to life in the room, if, before the contemplated deed is committed, the person turns with remorse to repent for the premeditated crime. The Lord also raises to life the corpse of a youth laid out for burial and, when he is revived, restores him to his weeping mother, that is, to the grieving Church. This happens when a person has committed a crime before being buried, that is, before being overcome by habit, provided that the person returns to repentance by belated remorse after condemning his offenses.

But why do I speak about corpses which are hidden or buried? Our Lord and Savior despises neither those who are buried nor those who stink from rottenness. He even arouses those whom he has recalled to a better life by repentance, even though because of long habit they were rotting from the dreadful ugliness of their vices, as if they were in a tomb. He restores to a better life bodies which have been overwhelmed with the weight of sins as in a tomb, and he orders the corpse which was bound to be released from its restraints, that is, from its deadly ties. This is done provided that the sinner feels the weight of being pressed down and recognizes his corruption and foul smell.

For this reason, brothers and sisters, if the hidden desires of any sin rebuke anyone, that person should hasten to be aroused in the room of the heart, that is, before committing in deed that which is conceived in thought. If there is a person whose death has been clearly revealed to the public by mourning, that is, who has committed whatever sin was intended, that person should hurry and return to the restorer of life before being overwhelmed by the weight of the tomb and before beginning to stink from rottenness.

However the person should not despair, even though the long-standing weight of sins has buried one in a foul-smelling condition as in fetid death. By those other resurrections which were accomplished for our hope, the Lord promises that he will restore life to all who desire to rise again. The goodness of our Lord is no less wonderful in the mystery than in the

*Our Lord did not want to bring death to the human race through his birth. He became man so that humans whom he had created might not perish. He suffered cruel torments in order that he might free the unworthy from deserving punishments.*

deed, for he has seen to it that the remedies for those who are willing to be cured are greater than the dangers, and that the remedies for restoring health are stronger than the wounds.

Our Lord did not want to bring death to the human race through his birth. He became man so that humans whom he had created might not perish. He suffered cruel torments in order that he might free the unworthy from deserving punishments. He hung on the tree of death in order to make amends for the fault which was derived from the tree through disobedience. For this he died and descended into hell, in order to rescue from it the dead who were kept in hell under the restraint of sin. Overcoming death he came back bringing living loot, that is, he restored to the living the life of those who were dead. He was not content to have humanity recover through his resurrection only what it had lost by disobedience when being deceived by the poisonous inspiration of the serpent. For it was not right that God our Redeemer should give to those who have been redeemed by his death only what the hatred of the hostile deceiver had cunningly destroyed. The latter expelled human beings from their true country, the former brought them back; the one took away paradise, while the other restored heaven.

Just as the devil overcame his captives by death, which was himself, so our Lord, who is life, gave to the redeemed eternal life and a share in his heavenly kingdom. Then we may taunt the devil and boast in the Lord as we say what was spoken through the prophet: "O death, where is your victory? O death, where is your sting?" (1 Cor. 15:5)

The extent of the divine mercy has taken me quite far away from the present feast. However, it is connected in such a way that the nativity could not be preached without the passion, nor could the passion without the glory of the nativity. Christ was born in order that he might suffer, he suffered in order that he might die, he died in order that he might descend into hell, he descended there in order that he might free the dead.

Although as God he was incapable of suffering, by uniting the substance of a human being with his divinity he humbled himself in such a way that, although God, he was born as a man and as man he arose again to God by triumphing over death. For this reason, dear brothers and sisters, the way came to those who were wandering, the judge came to the guilty, the physician came to those who were sick, life came to the dead.

Why? Because without the way the pilgrim could not return to his true country, without a judge the guilty could not be forgiven, and without life the dead could not be revived. Therefore we have a way of return on the road, mercy in our judge, a remedy in sickness, and deliverance in death. The

*However, it is connected in such a way that the nativity could not be preached without the passion, nor could the passion without the glory of the nativity.*

way by which we can arise came down to us, the judge came to rebuke death and to free humanity, the physician came to remove infirmities and to grant endless health to the sick, life came to descend into hell, in order that it might free the dead from it by killing death.

O Lord, with what joy and exultation shall we describe the benefits of such great goodness? What more is there that we who are sick might ask than what you have offered of your own accord to those who did not deserve it? And yet we poor sinners also plead with you to love in us what you bore for us. If only we might love our own life in the same way that you concede to love your death in us.

Therefore, dear brothers and sisters, let us love our price and let us make ourselves worthy of it by good deeds and right actions, since through the death of our Lord we have been worthy to be redeemed and even freed. For this reason, too, let us keep our life pure and undefiled for our Lord and Redeemer as it was entrusted to us. As we joyfully celebrate the feast of his nativity, with his help may we strive to live in such a way that such great and immense benefits of our God may not bring us judgment but may lead to our profit, because he himself is worthy of it, who lives and reigns with the Father.

# HARK! A THRILLING VOICE IS SOUNDING

A text translated from tenth-century manuscripts that may date back to the fifth century. This English text is based on a translation from *Hymns Ancient and Modern* (1861).

*Hark! A thrilling voice is sounding!*
*"Christ is near," we hear it say.*
*"Cast away the works of darkness,*
*All you children of the day!"*

*Startled at the solemn warning,*
*From the darkness we arise;*
*Christ, our sun, all ill dispelling,*
*Shines upon the morning skies.*

*See, the Lamb so long expected*
*Comes with pardon down from heaven.*
*Let us haste, with tears of sorrow,*
*One and all, to be forgiven;*

*So when next he comes in glory*
*And the world is wrapped in fear,*
*He will shield us with his mercy*
*And with words of love draw near.*

*Honor, glory, might, dominion*
*To the Father and the Son,*
*With the ever-living Spirit*
*While eternal ages run.*

# 5

## Gregory the Great,
## 540–604

*G*regory the Great lived during the transition *from the patristic to medieval periods. He reflects the theological vision of the early medieval period, helping us understand how the legacy of earlier theologians, such as Augustine, persisted after their death. He is also considered the first of the medieval popes. Gregorian chant is named after him, probably by later liturgical editors who wanted to legitimize their work by associating it with his strong reputation. His writings include works on pastoral ministry, biographies of earlier Christians, biblical expositions, and sermons.*

*Gregory's sermons come to us in three principal collections—sermons on Job, on Ezekiel, and for festal days. He preached this sermon on Matthew 2 early in his pontificate at Rome. Like many of Gregory's sermons, this*

*one focuses on small details in the text, such as the star,
and the unique meaning of gold, frankincense, and myrrh.
The concern for the meaning of each element of the Magi's
gifts was not new with Gregory and is found in several
works from the early church, including Augustine's.
Gregory gathers up these details in his creation-oriented
pronouncement that "all the elements bore witness that
their creator had come." The sermon ends with a call to
penitence—an important theme in Gregory's writing and
preaching that would set the stage for the very penitential
piety of later centuries.*

∿ ∾

As you have heard in the lesson from the Gospel (Matt.
2:1–12), dearly beloved, when the king of heaven was born,
a king on earth was alarmed. Earthly pride is undoubtedly
alarmed when the Highness of heaven is revealed.

But we must ask what it means that when our Redeemer
was born, an angel appeared to the shepherds in Judea,
and a star and not an angel guided the Magi from the east
to worship him. This was the reason: a reasoning being,
an angel, preached to the Jews as persons capable of using

> *. . . when the king of heaven was born,
> a king on earth was alarmed. Earthly pride
> is undoubtedly alarmed when the Highness
> of heaven is revealed.*

their reason, but a sign and not a voice guided the Gentiles,
who did not know how to make use of reason to know the
Lord. For this reason Paul says: "Prophecy has been given for
believers not for unbelievers, but signs have been given for
unbelievers and not for believers." (1 Cor. 14:22) And so prophecy
has been given to the Jews as believers and not unbelievers,

and signs have been given to the Gentiles as unbelievers and not believers. And we must note that the apostles preached our Redeemer to these same Gentiles when he was already a grown man, but a star declared him to the Gentiles when he was a small child, not yet able to perform the normal human function of speaking. It was surely reasonable both that preachers should make the speaking Lord known to us by speaking, and silent elements should preach him when he was not yet speaking.

But with all these signs that were displayed when the Lord was born or when he died, we must note the great hardness of heart of some of the Jewish people. They failed to recognize him either by the gift of prophecy or by his miracles. In truth all the elements bore witness that their creator had come. Indeed, to speak of them in a human way, the heavens knew that he was God because they immediately sent out a star, the sea knew him because it allowed him to walk on it; (Matt. 14:25) the earth knew him because it trembled when he died; the sun knew him because it hid the rays of its light; the stones and walls of houses knew him because

*It was surely reasonable both that preachers should make the speaking Lord known to us by speaking, and silent elements should preach him when he was not yet speaking.*

they were broken at the time of his death; the lower world recognized him because it gave up the dead it was holding; (Matt. 27:45–53) and yet the hearts of the Jews remained full of unbelief, and did not know that he was God, although all the dumb elements perceived him as Lord. Harder than stones, they were unwilling to be broken for repentance, and they refused to acknowledge him whom, as I have said, the elements proclaimed to be God either by their signs or being broken.

Their condemnation is greater because they despised when he was born the one they had long known would be born. And they knew not only that he would be born, but even where he was to be born. For on being asked by Herod, they named the place of his birth as they had learned it from the authority of the scriptures, and they testified that Bethlehem was to be honored by the birth of their new leader. Therefore their very knowledge was for them a testimony for their condemnation, and for us a help towards belief. Isaac blessing his son Jacob (Gen. 27:27–29) foreshadowed them well. For his eyesight was dim and he prophesied, not seeing his son who was present, but foreseeing many things for him in the future. Surely the Jewish people too were filled with the spirit of prophecy, and blind. They foretold many future things about him whom they did not recognize when he was present.

But when Herod knew of the birth of our king, he resorted to clever arguments to prevent being deprived of his earthly kingdom. He demanded that it be reported to him where the child was to be found. He pretended that he wished to worship him, in order to destroy him if he could find him. But what use is human hatred against the divine plan? "There is no wisdom, no insight, no plan that can succeed against the LORD." (Prov. 21:30) The star which had appeared to them guided the Magi on. They found the new-born king and offered him their gifts; and they were warned in a dream not to return to Herod. And so Herod was unable to find Jesus, whom he was seeking. Who are foreshadowed in Herod but the hypocrites, who when they falsely seek the Lord never deserve to find him?

At this point we should know that the heretical followers of Priscillian consider that every individual person is born under the influence of the stars. They claim in support of their error that a new star shone forth when the Lord appeared in a human body, a star which they believe influenced his destiny. But we must consider the words of the Gospel. It is said of the star, "Until it came to rest over the place where the child was." (Matt. 2:9) It was not the child who was drawn to the star, but the star to the child; if you allow me to say so, the star did not influence the destiny of the child, but the child influenced the destiny of the star by his appearance. But let no talk about destiny come near the hearts of believers. Only the creator, who made human beings, directs their lives. Human beings were not made for the sake of the stars, but stars for the sake of human beings. If a star is called the destiny of someone, that person is said to be subject to its control. When Jacob came out of his mother's womb holding his elder brother's heel in his hand, (Gen. 25:25–26) the elder couldn't have emerged completely without the younger having begun to follow him out. And yet even though their mother gave birth at the same time to both of them, their lives did not turn out the same. But the astrologers are accustomed to answer this by saying that the power of the constellations is instantaneous. I, on the contrary, say that a birth takes some time. Therefore if the position of the stars changes in a moment, it will then be necessary for them to say that there are as many destinies as there are body parts. The astrologers also typically say that whoever is born under the sign of Aquarius is destined to the occupation of a fisherman in this life. But people say that Gaetulia [a city in what is now Morocco—Ed.] has no fishermen. Would anyone say that where there are no fishermen no one is born under the sign of Aquarius? They also declare that persons born under the sign of Libra will be bankers; and there are parts of many countries that do not have bankers. They must therefore admit either that this sign of the Zodiac does not exist among them, or that it has no influence there on people's destinies. Moreover, in the territories of the Persians and the Franks kings are hereditary. As they are being born, who can say how many slaves are being born at exactly the same moment? The sons of kings are born under the same sign as the sons of slaves, and go on to rule, while the slaves who are born with them die in slavery. I have said this briefly about the star so that I should not appear to have passed over the foolishness of the astrologers in silence.

The Magi brought gold, incense, and myrrh. Gold is fitting for a king; incense is offered in sacrifice to God; the bodies of the dead are embalmed with myrrh. Therefore the Magi, with their mystical gifts, also preach him whom they

> *Gold is fitting for a king; incense is offered in sacrifice to God; the bodies of the dead are embalmed with myrrh.*

worshiped, a king with the gold, God with the incense, a human being with the myrrh.

- There are some heretics who believe that he is God, but do not believe that he rules everywhere. They indeed offer him incense, but are unwilling to offer him gold as well.
- There are some who think that he is king but deny that he is God. These offer him gold but are unwilling to offer him incense.
- There are some who say that he is both God and king but deny that he took to himself a human body. These certainly offer him gold and incense, but they are unwilling to offer him the myrrh of the humanity that he assumed.

Likewise,

- Let us also offer *gold* to the Lord who has been born, that we may say that he rules everywhere.
- Let us offer *incense*, that we may believe that he who appeared in time existed as God before time.

- Let us offer *myrrh*, that we may believe that he, who in his divinity is unable to suffer, was a human being with a body like ours.

There is something more that can be understood by the gold, incense and myrrh.

- Solomon testifies that *gold* symbolizes wisdom when he says, "A pleasing treasure lies in the mouth of the wise man." (Prov. 21:20 LXX)
- The psalmist bears witness that *incense* offered to God expresses the power of prayer when he says, "Let my prayer ascend as incense in your sight." (Ps. 141:2)
- The *myrrh* indicates the putting to death of our bodies; therefore holy Church says of its workers who strive even unto death on God's behalf, "My hands dripped with myrrh." (Song 5:5)

And so,

- We too offer *gold* to the new-born king if we shine in his sight with the brightness of the wisdom from on high.
- We offer him *incense* if we enkindle on the altar of our hearts the thoughts of our human minds by our holy pursuit of prayer, so as to give forth a sweet smell to God by our heavenly desire.
- We offer him *myrrh* if we put to death the vices of our bodies by our self-denial.

As I have said, myrrh prevents dead bodies from decomposing. For a dead body to decompose is the same as for our human body to become a slave to the decay of immorality, as is said of some by the prophet, "The pack animals have decomposed in their own dung." (Joel 1:17) Truly pack animals decompose in their own dung when fleshly-minded persons end their lives in the stench of immorality. Therefore we are offering myrrh to God when we use the spice of self-restraint to keep this earthly body of ours from decomposing through immorality.

The Magi indicate something important to us by their returning to their own country by another way. By doing what they were advised to do they suggest to us what we should do. Paradise is our country. We are forbidden to return to it, once we have known Jesus, by the way by which he came. Indeed we left our country by being proud, by being disobedient, by pursuing visible things, by tasting forbidden food; we must return to it by weeping, by being obedient, by rejecting visible things and by curbing our bodily appetites. And so we return to our country by another way: pleasure led us away from the joys of paradise, sorrows summon us to return.

Therefore, dearly beloved, we must always be fearful and alert, setting before the eyes of our hearts on the one hand the sinfulness of our works, and on the other the severity of the final judgment. Consider how severe a judge is coming.

*Let us punish our sins with tears, and . . .*
*let us anticipate his presence*
*by admitting our guilt.*

He threatens sinners with terrors, and yet he still bears with them; and he puts off coming for this reason, that he may find fewer to condemn. Let us punish our sins with tears, and with the voice of the psalmist let us anticipate his presence by admitting our guilt. (Ps. 95:2)

Don't be deceived by captivating pleasures, don't be led astray by barren joys. The judge who said, "Woe to you who laugh now, because you will mourn and weep," (Luke 6:25) is near. Solomon says in this regard: "Laughter will be mingled with sorrow, and mourning follows at the end of joy;" (Prov. 14:3) and again: "I have accounted laughter as an error and said to joy, Why do you deceive for no good reason?" (Qoh. 2:2) and again: "The heart of the wise is where there is sadness, and the heart of fools where there is happiness." (Qoh. 7:4)

Let us fear the commandments of God if we would truly celebrate a feast of God. Distress over sin is a pleasing sacrifice to God, according to the psalmist who says: "An afflicted spirit is a sacrifice to God." (Ps. 51:17) Our past sins were forgiven when we received baptism; since baptism we have committed many sins, even though we cannot be cleansed again by the water of baptism. Therefore because we have corrupted our lives even after baptism, let us baptize our conscience with our tears. Since we are seeking our country again by another way, let us who departed from it flippantly return to it in bitter anger at our sins. Let us do this with the help of our Lord, who lives and reigns with the Father in the unity of the Holy Spirit, God for ever and ever. Amen.

# O SPLENDOR OF GOD'S GLORY BRIGHT

Based on a Latin hymn by Ambrose of Milan, as testified by Fulgentius, bishop of Ruspe, North Africa, and Bede. This English text is based on a translation by Louis F. Benson (1910).

O Splendor of God's glory bright,
From light eternal bringing light,
O Light of light, light's living Spring,
True Day, all days illumining.

Come, very Sun of Heaven's love,
In lasting radiance from above,
And pour the Holy Spirit's ray
On all we think or do today.

And now to You our prayers ascend,
O Father, glorious without end;
We plead with Sovereign Grace for powers
To conquer in temptation's hour.

Confirm our will to do the right,
And keep our hearts from envy's blight;
Let faith her eager fires renew,
And hate the false, and love the true.

O joyful be the passing day
With thoughts as pure as morning's ray,
With faith like noontide shining bright,
Our souls unshadowed by the night.

Dawn's glory gilds the earth and skies,
Let him, our perfect Morn, arise,
The Word in God the Father one,
The Father imaged by the Son!

# 6

## Bede,
## 673—735

*ede, later given the title "Venerable Bede," lived in what is now England. He is sometimes called the father of English history for his biographies of several Christian leaders and for his* Ecclesiastical History of the English People, *completed in 731. He was a careful student in many disciplines, with a particular interest in earlier biblical commentaries.*

*This sermon is taken from a large cycle of sermons for the entire Christian Year. It explores the Christmas message from the gospel of Matthew, dwelling especially on the significance of the virgin birth.*

*Alert readers will notice references to the "perpetual virginity" of Mary, an idea that dates back to a treatise written by Jerome in A.D. 383 that in time was widely taught by both Catholic and Orthodox churches, and much disputed by Protestant theologians.*

~ ~

In a very brief but true teaching, the evangelist Matthew described the nativity of our Lord and Savior Jesus Christ, the nativity by which the Son of God, eternal before the ages, appeared in time as the Son of Man. After Matthew has led us through the generations of Christ's ancestors from Abraham to Joseph, Mary's husband, and showed that they all, by the typical manner of human creation, were born as well as produced children, (Matt. 1:1–17) he then wishes to speak of Mary herself. He makes clear what a difference there was between her child-bearing and that of the rest. The rest were produced by the normal union of a male and a female. Jesus, however, seeing that he was Son of God, was to be born into the world by a virgin. It was entirely fitting that when God wished to become a human being, for the sake of human beings, he be born of none other than a virgin. When the Virgin bears a child, she bears no other son than one who is God.

"His mother Mary was pledged to be married to Joseph, but before they came together, she was found to be with child through the Holy Spirit." The evangelist Luke explains sufficiently in what order of events and in what city the conception took place. Since your reverences certainly know this well, something must be said about a few of the things that Matthew wrote. We should note first that in stating "before they came together," what is suggested by the verb "come together" is not actual sleeping together. It is the period of marriage which customarily preceded the time when she who had been pledged started to be a wife. Therefore before they came together, before they celebrated the solemnities of marriage with suitable ceremony, "she was found to be with child through the Holy Spirit." According to the order of the story, they afterwards "came together" when Joseph, at the angel's command, received his wife, but they did not sleep together, for there follows, "but he had no union with her." She was discovered to be pregnant by Joseph alone. Through the privilege of marriage he knew almost everything about his future wife, and so by close observation he soon noticed that she was expecting a child.

Then Matthew says: "Because Joseph her husband was a righteous man and did not want to expose her to public disgrace, he had in mind to divorce her quietly." Joseph saw that Mary had conceived, though he knew well that she had not been touched by any man. Since he was just and wished to do everything justly, he chose what seemed the best course of action: he would neither divulge this to others, nor receive her himself as his wife, but he would privately change the marriage proposal and allow her to remain in the position of a woman pledged to be married, as she was. Now he had read in Isaiah that a virgin of the house of David would conceive and give birth to the Lord, and he also knew that Mary took her origin from this house, and so he did not disbelieve that this prophecy had been fulfilled in her. But if he had sent her away privately and not received her as his wife, and if she, as a woman pledged to be married, were to give birth, there would surely have been many people calling her a harlot rather than a virgin. For this reason Joseph all at once changed his mind, having a better idea. In order to preserve Mary's reputation, he would receive her as his wife, celebrating the marriage feast, but he would keep her virginity perpetually intact. For the Lord preferred that some people be ignorant of the manner of his birth rather than have them attack his mother's reputation.

Then Matthew says: "As Joseph was pondering these things, an angel of the Lord appeared to him in his dreams, saying, 'Joseph, son of David, do not be afraid to receive Mary as your wife, because what is conceived in her is from the Holy Spirit. She will give birth to a son and you are to give him the name Jesus, because he will save his people from their sins'." These words certainly teach the manner of his conception and the dignity of his birth: Mary would conceive through the Holy Spirit and give birth to the Christ. Although the angel did not explicitly name him Christ, he did, when explaining the meaning of the name Jesus, apply to him the words "Author of salvation" and "Savior of the people." In this way, the angel clearly indicated that Jesus was the Christ so that Joseph might learn what he had not known and might completely remove from his mind any thought of union with God's mother. However, through God's righteous and necessary plan, Joseph was ordered to receive Mary as his wife, but only in name, so that she would not be stoned as an adulteress by the Jews.

In addition, when fleeing to Egypt, she would be comforted by a man who, with a husband's care, would guard her as a powerless female and testify to her perpetual virginity. Catholic interpreters also provide other reasons why Joseph was to receive God's mother as his wife, and one who wishes will find these in their writings.

The evangelist also uses a prophet's prediction of the virgin birth in order that such a majestic miracle might be more certainly believed than if he alone had proclaimed it. Now it is usual for Matthew to affirm everything that he says with prophetic testimonies. For he wrote his gospel especially for the sake of Jews who had come to believe, but who, although they were reborn in Christ, were not able to be torn away from the ceremonies of the law. Therefore he attempted to raise them from the fleshly sense of the law and the prophets to the spiritual sense, which concerns Christ, so that they might more securely attain the sacraments of the Christian faith to the extent that they acknowledged that these were nothing other than those which the prophets had predicted.

"A virgin will be with child and give birth to a son, and will call Emmanuel, which means 'God with us.'" Because of the Savior's name, he is called "God with us" by the prophet. (Isa. 7:14) The name expresses both natures of his one person. Born from the Father before time, he is God himself in the fullness of time. He became Emmanuel (that is, "God with us") in his mother's womb because he considerately took the weakness of our nature into the unity of his person when "the Word became flesh and made his dwelling among us." (John 1:14) In a wonderful manner he began to be what we are, while continuing to be what he had been, assuming our nature in such a way that he himself would not lose what he had been.

"When Joseph woke up, he did what the angel of the Lord had commanded him and accepted his wife and had no union with her." He accepted her as his wife in name for the reasons which we mentioned above, and he had no union with her because of the hidden mysteries which he had learned. But if anyone wishes to oppose this explanation of ours and to contend that the blessed mother of God was never, by the celebration of marriage, taken by Joseph as a wife in name, let him explain this place in the holy gospel better. At the same time let him show that the Jews allowed anyone to be united in flesh with the woman to whom he was pledged; then we will be persuaded by his interpretation—only we may not believe that anything at all took place for which public opinion could disgrace the mother of the Lord.

Moreover, no one should suppose that what the evangelist adds, "until she gave birth to her first-born son," should be

*In a wonderful manner he began to be what we are, while continuing to be what he had been, assuming our nature in such a way that he himself would not lose what he had been.*

understood as though after her son was born Joseph did have union with her, an opinion that some have perversely held. For you brothers ought to be aware that because the evangelist said, "He had no union with her until she gave birth to her son," some heretics have believed that Joseph did have union with Mary after the Lord was born and from that union were born those whom scripture calls the brothers of the Lord. (e.g. Matt. 13:55) As a support for their error they use this passage, which applies the term "first-born" to the Lord. May God turn this blasphemy away from the faith of us all, and may he make us understand according to the entire church's piety that our Savior's parents were always distinguished by their perfect virginity and that, as is typical in the scriptures, the term "brothers of the Lord" is applied not to their children but to their relatives.

May he also make us understand that the evangelist was not careful to say whether Joseph had union with her after the Son of God was born because he did not imagine that anyone would dispute it. Since they were given the unusual grace of having a son born to them while they remained in the pure state of virginity, they could not in any way break the rules of purity and pollute the exceedingly holy temple of God with the seed of their corruption. Also we should note that "first-born" are not, as the heretics believe, only those who come before other siblings, but, according to the authority of scripture, they are all those who first open the womb, whether some siblings follow them or not.

However, it can be understood that, for a special reason, the Lord was said to be first-born. For, in the Apocalypse, John refers to him as he "who is the faithful witness, the first-born of the dead and the prince of the kings of the earth." (Rev. 1:5) And the apostle Paul says, "Now those whom he has foreknown he has also predestined to become conformed to the image of his Son, that he himself might be the first-born among many brothers." (Rom. 8:29) He is first-born among many brothers because "to as many as received him he gave the power to become sons of God." (John 1:12) He is appropriately called the first-born of these brothers because in honor he came before all the sons of adoption, (Eph. 1:5) even those who were born before the time of his incarnation. Therefore, they can very truly bear witness with John, "He who comes after us was before us." (John 1:15) In other words, "He was born into the world after us, but because of his worthy virtue and kingdom he is appropriately called the first-born of us all."

Also in his own divine nativity he can appropriately be said to be first-born because, prior to begetting any other creature by making it, the Father begot a Son coeternal with himself; and prior to begetting any other sons of adoption for himself by redeeming them through the Word of truth, the eternal Father begot a Word coeternal to himself. Therefore, the Word himself, the very Son of God, his virtue and wisdom, says,

"I came forth from the mouth of the Most High, first-born before every creature." (Sir. 24:5) Mary gave birth to her first-born son, that is, the son of her substance; she gave birth to him who was also born God from God before every creature, and in that humanity in which he was created he truly "went before" every creature.

"And Joseph gave him the name Jesus." "Jesus" in Hebrew means "saving" or, in Latin, "savior." It is certainly clear that the prophets called upon his name, for the following are sung out of a deep desire for a vision of him: "My soul will rejoice in the LORD and delight in his salvation." (Ps. 35:9) "My soul faints with longing for your salvation." (Ps. 119:81) "Yet I will glory in the LORD; I will rejoice in God my Jesus." (Hab. 3:18) And especially that verse: "Save me, O God, by your name!" (Ps. 54:1) as if the prophet is saying: "You who are called Savior, make bright the glory of your name in me by saving me."

"Jesus" is the name of the Son who was born of a virgin, and, as the angel explained, this name meant that he would save his people from their sins. (Matt. 1:21) Certainly he who saves from sins is the same one who will save from the corruption of mind and body which happen as a result of sins.

"Christ" is a term of priestly and royal dignity, for in the law priests and kings were called "christs," from "chrism," that is, an anointing with holy oil. And he who appeared in the world as true king and high priest they called Christ, and he was anointed with the oil of gladness, setting him above those who shared his anointing. (Ps. 45:7; Heb. 1:9) From this anointing, that is, the chrism, he himself is called "Christ," and those who share this anointing, that is, spiritual grace, are called "Christians."

Since he is Savior, may he considerately save us from sins. Since he is high priest, may he considerately reconcile us to God the Father. Since he is king, may he considerately give us the eternal kingdom of his Father, Jesus Christ our Lord, who with the Father and the Holy Spirit lives and reigns, God for all ages. Amen.

# CREATOR OF THE STARS OF NIGHT

From a medieval Latin hymn for evening prayer. This English text includes selected stanzas, based on a translation by John Mason Neale (1851).

*Creator of the stars of night,*
*Your people's everlasting light,*
*O Christ, Redeemer of us all,*
*We pray You, hear us when we call.*

*When this old world drew on toward night,*
*You came, but not in splendor bright,*
*Not as a monarch, but the child*
*Of Mary, blameless mother mild.*

*At Your great name, O Jesus, now*
*All knees must bend, all hearts must bow:*
*All things on earth with one accord,*
*Like those in heaven, shall call You Lord.*

*To God the Father, God the Son,*
*And God the Spirit, Three in One,*
*Praise, honor, might and glory be*
*From age to age eternally.*

# 7

## Rabanus Maurus of Mainz,
## ca. 780–ca. 856

*S*ometimes called Praeceptor Germaniae
("Teacher of Germany"), Rabanus Maurus served the
church in two long careers—first, for twenty years
as a director of an abbey school, and then, for twenty
years as bishop of Mainz. He was a student of Alcuin and
had access to the best learning of his time. His writings
include two sermon cycles, several biblical commentaries,
and writings on several pastoral issues.

   This Christmas sermon, like many of his sermons, is
filled with exhortations and pleas for obedience. One can
sense here the kind of works-oriented piety that was the
primary concern of later Reformers. At the same time,
his call for obedience is grounded in an understanding
that we obey "only with God's help"; and it is conveyed
with evocative and luminous language that invites, rather

*than shames, worshipers to true obedience: "Let your*
*souls gleam with purity, shine in love, be bright with acts*
*of charity, glow with righteousness and humility, dazzle,*
*before all else, with love of God."*

᯽ ᯽

As that most holy festival is now approaching on which
our Savior mercifully gave himself to be born among human
beings, take care, dear brothers and sisters, to note how
we ought to be ready for the advent of such great power.
We should be prepared joyfully and gladly to deserve to
receive our King and Lord with glory and praise, and in his
sight amid the happy crowds of the saints to rejoice with
thanksgiving rather than, rejected by him on account of our
uncleanness, to deserve eternal damnation among sinners.
Therefore, I beg and advise that, as much as we can, we
labor with God's help, so that on that day with sincere and
pure conscience, clean of heart and pure of body, we can
approach the Lord's altar and receive his body and blood,
not to our judgment but for the cure of our souls.

For our life resides in Christ's body. The Lord himself has
said, "Unless you eat the flesh of the Son of Man, and drink
his blood, you will not have life in you." (John 6:53) Let any
who wish to have life change their life, then; for if anyone
does not change a life of sin, so as to live righteously, that
person will receive the true life which is Christ's body to
his judgment. He will be made corrupt from it rather than
whole, put to death rather than restored to life.

For the apostle said: "Whoever eats the Lord's body and
drinks his blood in an unworthy manner, eats and drinks
judgment to oneself." (1 Cor. 11:27) And though it is always
appropriate for us to be gloriously clothed in good works,
nevertheless, on the Lord's birthday particularly, there is this
obligation, as he himself says in the Gospel (Matt. 5:16) that

our good works ought to shine before others so that in all things God may be glorified.

Consider this, brothers and sisters: If an earthly king or the head of some great family should invite you to his birthday party, what kind of clothes would you be anxious to wear when you go, how new, how neat, how elegant, so that the eye of your host would not be offended by their age, their shabbiness, or their dirtiness. Therefore, in this same way, strive zealously—as much as you can, Christ being your helper—that your souls may be decorated by the various

*Let your souls gleam with purity,*
*shine in love, be bright with acts of charity,*
*glow with righteousness and humility, dazzle,*
*before all else, with love of God.*

ornaments of virtues, adorned with the gems of simplicity and the flowers of sobriety, with clear conscience, when they go to the birthday celebrations of the Eternal, that is, of the Lord our Savior. Let your souls gleam with purity, shine in love, be bright with acts of charity, glow with righteousness and humility, dazzle, before all else, with love of God.

For the Lord Christ, should he see you so well-dressed celebrating his birthday, will come himself, and not only to visit your souls but even to remain there and to dwell in them, as it is written: "For this reason, I will come and live and move among them and they will be my people, and I will be their God," says the Lord God. (2 Cor. 6:16; Gen. 17:8) O how happy is that soul which is brought by good works to receive Christ as guest and inhabitant, ever happy, ever joyful, ever glad, and free from every dread of vices! By contrast, how unhappy is that conscience which stains itself with evil deeds so that Christ does not begin to rest in it but the devil begins to rule in it! Such a soul, if the healing of repentance does not come quickly, is abandoned by the light and seized by shadows; emptied of sweetness, filled with bitterness; invaded by death, separated from life.

Nevertheless, do not let such a soul despair of the Lord's goodness, nor be broken by deadly despair, but let it quickly return to repentance, and while the wounds of its sins are fresh and still inflamed, may it make use of the wholesome ointment of its tears, because our Physician is omnipotent, and is used to healing our stripes so that no trace of scars remains.

Only let us have faith in him, and let us continue in good works as much as we can and never despair of his mercy. Therefore, my dear brothers and sisters, always reflecting on these things, let those who are good strive to continue with God's grace in good works, because, not the one who

*O how happy is that soul which is brought by good works to receive Christ as guest and inhabitant, ever happy, ever joyful, ever glad, and free from every dread of vices!*

begins, but "the one who endures to the end will be saved." (Matt. 10:22)

But those who know that they are slow to give alms, ready to become angry, inclined to lust, let them, with the Lord's aid, hurry to rescue themselves from evils, so that they may deserve to fulfill what is good, so that, when the Day of Judgment comes, they may not be punished with the wicked and sinners, but may deserve to arrive with the righteous and the merciful at the rewards that are eternal, under the protection of our Lord Jesus Christ, who with the Father and the Holy Spirit lives and reigns forever and ever. Amen.

# A GREAT
# AND MIGHTY WONDER

A Greek hymn for Christmas Eve by Germanus (ca. 634–734). The English text is based on a translation by John Mason Neale (1861).

*A great and mighty wonder,*
*A full and holy cure:*
*The virgin bears the infant*
*With virgin honor pure!*

> *Repeat the hymn again:*
> *"To God on high be glory*
> *And peace on earth to men!"*

*The Word becomes incarnate*
*And yet remains on high,*
*And cherubim sing anthems*
*To shepherds from the sky.*

*While thus they sing your Monarch,*
*Those bright angelic bands,*
*Rejoice, O vales and mountains,*
*And oceans, clap your hands.*

*Since all he comes to ransom,*
*By all be he adored,*
*The infant born in Bethlehem,*
*The Savior and the Lord.*

~ SERMON ~

# 8

## Guerric of Igny,
### 1070—1160

uerric of Igny was born and educated at
Tournai (in what is now Belgium), and became the
schoolmaster of the cathedral school. Later he went
to Clairvaux, where Bernard encouraged him to take
monastic vows. For the last twenty years of his life, he
served as the Abbot of the Cistercian monastery in Igny.

Guerric's Christmas sermon is a thoughtful meditation
on the meaning of the Christmas gospel that returns
repeatedly to the importance of spiritual perception or
sight. Guerric gives special attention to specific virtues or
fruits of the gospel, including joy, justice, humility, and
faith, that arise from devotion to Jesus Christ.

~ ~

You have come together, brothers and sisters, to hear the Word of God. But God has provided something better for us. Today we have been granted not only to hear but also to see the Word of God, if only "we will make our way to Bethlehem and see the Word which the Lord has made and shown to us." (Luke 2:15) God knew that human minds were incapable of perceiving invisible things, unwilling to be taught about the things of heaven, slow to yield their faith unless the object itself in which they were asked to believe was visibly displayed to the senses so as to convince them. For although faith comes from hearing (Rom. 10:17) it comes much

*Today we have been granted not only to hear but also to see the Word of God.*

more readily and promptly from sight, as we are taught by the example of him who was told: "Because you have seen me you have believed," (John 20:29) you who were unbelieving when you heard. Because it is more difficult to believe in what is only heard, not seen, the faith of those who have not seen is rightly declared blessed by the Lord, because they have attributed more to the authority of the Word than to the experience of their own senses or reason.

Yet God wishes to satisfy our slowness in everything. His Word, which previously he had made to be heard, today he makes visible to us, indeed even tangible. So some of us could say: "Our message concerns that Word, who is life; what he was from the beginning, what we have heard about him, what our own eyes have seen of him; what it was that met our gaze and the touch of our hands." (1 John 1:1) He was from the beginning of that eternity which is without a beginning; we heard him promised from the beginning of time; we saw him and handled him shown to us at the end of time.

Elsewhere you will find that the Word of God has been made not only an object of sight and touch but also of taste and smell. (Ps. 33:11; Song 4:11) He sought an entrance for himself to the soul through all the ways of the senses, so that as death had entered through the senses life too might return through the same. If then the Word was made flesh (John 1:14) it was for us who are wholly flesh, so that as we had previ-

> *If then the Word was made flesh it was*
> *for us who are wholly flesh, so that as we*
> *had previously been able to hear the Word*
> *of God, we might now be able to see him and*
> *taste him made flesh, summoning all the senses*
> *to bear witness to our hearing.*

ously been able to hear the Word of God, we might now be able to see him and taste him made flesh, summoning all the senses to bear witness to our hearing. All our senses should confess with one agreement and one voice: "As we heard, so we have seen." (Ps. 47:9)

Yet incomparably more is now granted to sight than was ever granted to hearing. Now the Word which is God (John 1:1) is seen, whereas before it was considered extraordinary to hear any word which came from God. As for the word which comes from God, brothers and sisters, I have on occasion seen it heard without interest. But surely the Word which is God can only be seen with joy. I will pass sentence on myself first: when the Word which is God offers himself to me today to be seen in that which I am, if it does not gladden me I am godless, if it does not edify me I am reprobate.

If then anyone is found among us who is troubled with spiritual sluggishness, I wish that the ears of such a person would not be wearied any longer by our contemptible sermon. Let the person journey to Bethlehem and there look on that Word of God which the angels eagerly desire to look on, (1 Peter 1:12) that Word which the Lord has shown to

⌐ *Proclaiming the* CHRISTMAS GOSPEL ⌐

us. (Luke 2:15) Let the person mentally picture what the living and creative (Heb. 4:12) Word of God is like as he lies there

*If then anyone is found among us who is troubled with spiritual sluggishness, I wish that the ears of such a person would not be wearied any longer by our contemptible sermon.*

in the manger. If only piety enlightens the eye of one who looks, what can there be so delightful to see, so wholesome to think about? What so edifies behavior, strengthens hope, inflames charity?

Truly it is a trustworthy word and deserving of every welcome, (1 Tim. 1:15) your almighty Word, Lord, which in such deep silence made its way down from the Father's royal throne (Wis. 18:14f.) into the mangers of animals and meanwhile speaks to us better by its silence. Let anyone who has ears to hear, hear (Matt. 11:15) what this loving and mysterious silence of the eternal Word speaks to us. For, unless hearing deceives me, among the other things which he speaks he speaks peace for the holy people (Ps. 84:9) on whom reverence for him and his example impose a religious silence.

And it was quite appropriately imposed. For what recommends the discipline of silence with such weight and such authority, what checks the evil of restless tongues and the storms of words, as the Word of God silent in the midst of humans? There is no word on my tongue, (Ps. 138:4) the almighty Word seems to confess while he is subject to his mother. (Luke 2:51) What madness then will prompt us to say: "With our tongues we can do great things; our lips are good friends to us; we own no master." (Ps. 11:5) If I were allowed I would gladly be mute and be brought low, and be silent even about good things, (Ps. 38:3) so that I might be able more attentively and diligently to apply my ear to the secret utterances and sacred meaning of this divine silence, learning in silence in the school of the Word if only for as long as the Word himself was silent under the instruction of his mother.

O brothers and sisters, if we listen reverently and diligently to this word which the Lord has made and shown to us today, (Luke 2:15) how much and how easily we can be

*Let anyone who has ears to hear,*
*hear what this loving and mysterious*
*silence of the eternal Word speaks to us.*

taught by it. It is an abbreviated word, yet in such a way that in it every word which makes for salvation is summed up: for it is "a word that sums up and abbreviates justly." (Rom. 9:28) And this abbreviated summing-up has overflowed with justice, as you remember was promised through Isaiah, since from its own fullness it has overflowed with justice on those who partake of it. (Isa. 10:22f.) Thus their justice may exceed that of the Scribes and Pharisees, (Matt. 5:20) even though these latter are busy practicing numerous justifications of the Law while the former are content with the brief and simple word of faith.

But is it surprising that the Word should have abbreviated all his words to us when he willed to be abbreviated himself and in a way diminished, to the point that he contracted himself from his incomprehensible immensity to the narrowness of the womb and he who contains the world suffered himself to be contained in a manger? In heaven this Word strikes awe into the angelic powers by his dreadful majesty; in the manger he feeds the simple and the stupid. There he is unsearchable to the keenest intellects of the angels; here he is to be touched by even the dull senses of human beings. Because God could not speak to us as spiritual but only carnal (1 Cor. 3:1) his Word was made flesh (John 1:14) so that all flesh might be able not only to hear but also

77

to see that the mouth of the Lord has spoken. (Isa. 40:5) And since in its wisdom the world did not know God's wisdom, by an unspeakable, voluntary descent from his dignity the same Wisdom of God made itself foolishness. (1 Cor. 1:21, 23) It offered itself to be learned by humans, however uneducated or stupid, and through the folly of preaching saved those who believed. (1 Cor. 1:21, 23) "I give you thanks, Father, Lord of heaven and earth, because you have hidden your wisdom from the wise and learned and revealed it to little ones. Even so, Father, so it was your good pleasure" (Matt. 11:25) that to little ones should be given the little one who is born for us. (Isa. 9:6)

The loftiness of the proud is too far removed from the humility of this little one. What is lofty among humans is detestable to him, who although he is truly lofty, has become a little one for us. It is only with little ones that this little one agrees, only in the humble and the quiet that he rests. Therefore as the little ones glory in him and sing: "A little one is born for us," (Isa. 9:6) so he too glories in them: "Here

> *. . . let us look with all earnestness upon this Word which has been made flesh, the immense God who has been made a little one.*

am I," he says, "and my children which God has given me." (Isa. 8:18; Heb. 2:13) For in order that the Father might give his little Son companions among those of his own age, the glory of martyrdom was at once inaugurated in the innocence of little ones before all others. (Matt. 1:16) By this the Holy Spirit intended us to understand that it is only to such little ones that the kingdom of heaven belongs. (Matt. 19:14)

If we wish to be made such little ones, again and again let us make our way to Bethlehem (Luke 2:15) and let us look with all earnestness upon this Word which has been made flesh, the immense God who has been made a little one.

In this visible and abbreviated Word (Isa. 10:23; Rom. 9:28) we may learn the Wisdom of God which in its entirety has been made humility. In this virtue that all-embracing Virtue has for the time being found its expression: that supreme Wisdom has willed for the time being to know nothing else but that humility of which he willed afterwards to declare himself a teacher. And he indeed—I say this to my own confusion—he, I say, was worthily and justly made a teacher of humility.

Although he knew humility well, by origin from his mother and naturally from his Father, nonetheless from the womb of his mother he learned it from the things he suffered. (Heb. 5:8) He was born in a travelers' inn in order that we might learn from his example and confess ourselves to be strangers and travelers on earth. (Heb. 11:13) In the travelers' inn too, he chose the last place and was put in a manger in order that we

*The whole pattern of a religious life seems already to have been born at his birth.*

might learn by this act what those words of David mean: "I chose to be unimportant in the house of my God rather than to dwell in the tents of sinners." (Ps. 84:10) He was wrapped in swaddling clothes (Luke 2:12) that we might be content to have just enough to cover us. (1 Tim. 6:8) In everything he was content with his mother's poverty and in everything he was subject to his mother. The whole pattern of a religious life seems already to have been born at his birth.

Blessed is the faith of the simple shepherds. Although it found an infant wrapped in swaddling clothes (Luke 2:12) it was not at all scandalized by them so as to refuse belief and think the less of him. Rather the devotion of their faith was increased so as to be more grateful for such an unspeakable, voluntary descent to us. For the more deeply humiliated and completely emptied out for them that majesty showed itself, the more easily and fully (if we wish to entertain a worthy opinion of them) love for him possessed and claimed their entire affections.

Brothers and sisters, you also will find today an infant wrapped in swaddling clothes and laid in the manger of the altar. Take care that the poverty of the covering does not offend or disturb the gaze of your faith as it perceives the reality of that exalted body beneath the appearance of other things. For as his mother Mary wrapped the infant in swaddling clothes, so our mother grace hides from us the reality of the same sacred body by covering it with certain outward appearances which are in keeping with the economy of salvation. So too mother wisdom covers the hidden majesty of the divine Word with riddles and figures, in order that in the one case the simplicity of faith and in the other the exercise of study may accumulate merit for itself unto salvation.

For when I too, brothers and sisters, declare to you in my own words the truth which is Christ, what else am I doing but wrapping Christ in remarkably humble swaddling clothes? Yet blessed is he to whom Christ is no lowlier even

*With complete devotion then let us think of Christ in the swaddling clothes with which his mother wrapped him, so that with eternal happiness we may see the glory and beauty with which his Father has clothed him, glory as of the Only-begotten of the Father, with whom and with the Holy Spirit may honor and glory be his forever and ever. Amen.*

in these swaddling clothes. A prudent man does not value precious merchandise less highly because it is packed in old sacking. Christ it is whom I desire to give you in my sermons, however poor they may be, so that according to the words of the apostle Peter you may enthrone him as Lord in your hearts. (1 Peter 3:15) Be patient and cherish that word planted in you which can bring salvation to your souls. (James 1:21) May all the wealth of Christ's world dwell in you, (Col. 3:16) love, that is, and remembrance of the incarnate Word, so that you may sing both happily and faithfully: "The Word was made flesh and lived among us." (John 1:14) With complete devotion then let us think of Christ in the swaddling clothes with which his mother wrapped him, so that with eternal happiness we may see the glory and beauty (Ps. 20:6) with which his Father has clothed him, glory as of the Only-begotten of the Father, (John 1:14) with whom and with the Holy Spirit may honor and glory be his forever and ever. Amen.

# O COME,
# O COME
# IMMANUEL

A twelfth-century hymn, based on earlier medieval prayers for the "O antiphons"—prayers that each identified a different name for the Messiah and that were prayed on the days leading up to Christmas. This English text is based on a translation by John Mason Neale (1851).

*O come, O come, Immanuel,*
*And ransom captive Israel*
*That mourns in lonely exile here*
*Until the Son of God appear.*

> *Rejoice! Rejoice! Immanuel*
> *Shall come to you, O Israel.*

*O come, O Wisdom from on high,*
*Who ordered all things mightily;*
*To us the path of knowledge show*
*And teach us in its ways to go.*

*O come, O come, great Lord of might,*
*Who to your tribes on Sinai's height*
*In ancient times did give the law*
*In cloud and majesty and awe.*

*O come, O Branch of Jesse's stem,*
*Unto your own and rescue them!*
*From depths of hell your people save,*
*And give them victory o'er the grave.*

*O come, O Key of David, come*
*And open wide our heavenly home.*
*Make safe for us the heavenward road*
*And bar the way to death's abode.*

*O come, O Bright and Morning Star,*
*And bring us comfort from afar!*
*Dispel the shadows of the night*
*And turn our darkness into light.*

*O come, O King of nations, bind*
*In one the hearts of all mankind.*
*Bid all our sad divisions cease*
*And be yourself our King of Peace.*

# 9

# Bernard of Clairvaux,
## 1090—1153

ernard of Clairvaux was an early leader in the Cistercian reform movement within medieval monasticism. The movement emphasized the spiritual disciplines, cultivated a deep piety, and resisted secular learning. Preaching was a key aspect of Cistercian spirituality, particularly preaching that features a straightforward presentation of the scriptural message clothed in deep devotion to God.

This sermon is built around the refrain "Jesus Christ, the Son of God, is born in Bethlehem of Judah." The first half of the sermon prompts listeners to wonder at the mystery of the incarnation; the second challenges worshipers to be ready to receive Jesus in a manner fitting to his coming.

↶ ↷

A voice of gladness has resounded in our land. In the dwellings of sinners a voice of joy and salvation has been heard. The good news has been announced, news of comfort, news full of rejoicing, worthy of all acceptance. Rejoice and give praise, O you mountains. All you trees of the forest applaud before the face of the Lord, for now he is coming. Hear, you heavens; and you, earth, give ear. Let the whole of creation be astounded and give praise; but you, O humans, above all others. For "Jesus Christ, the Son of God, is born in Bethlehem of Judah."

Who is so hard of heart that his soul does not soften at this news? What sweeter message could be proclaimed? What more delightful event could be announced? Has anything like this ever been heard before, has the world ever received such tidings? "Jesus Christ, the Son of God, is born in Bethlehem of Judah."

Only a few words about the Word who for us became little, but words full of heavenly sweetness. Our affection

*Our affection strives to pour out more abundantly its cup of tender delight, but can find no adequate expression.*

strives to pour out more abundantly its cup of tender delight, but can find no adequate expression. For such is the beauty of this message that if one iota is changed it begins to lose its flavor. "Jesus Christ, the Son of God, is born in Bethlehem of Judah."

O nativity, spotless in sanctity, worthy of all honor in the world, loved by people for the great benefit it grants them, unfathomable even to the angels for the depths of the sacred mystery it contains, utterly wonderful for the extraordinary excellence of such a novelty, for it is an event the like of which was never seen before, nor will ever have an imitation again. The only birth ever free from pain, a birth which did not stain but rather consecrated the temple of that virginal womb.

O birth far above nature, but for the benefit of nature, surpassing nature by the excellence of its great miracle, but restoring nature by the power of its mystery. Who shall worthily proclaim this new birth? An angel announces it; the power of the Most High casts a shadow; the Spirit comes upon a virgin; a virgin believes; by her faith a virgin conceives; a virgin gives birth to a child; she remains a virgin: who can

*The Word is born a child.*
*It is only right that we should be astounded.*

pretend not to be astounded? The Son of the Most High is born: God begotten of God before all time. The Word is born a child. It is only right that we should be astounded.

This birth has not been fruitless; it is not without effect that Majesty has humbly come. "Jesus Christ, the Son of God, is born in Bethlehem of Judah." You who are mere dust, awaken and give praise. Look, the Lord draws near, bringing to us salvation, perfumed ointments, and glory. For without salvation Jesus cannot come; without ointments Christ, the Anointed, cannot come; without glory the Son of God cannot come; for he himself is salvation, and anointment, and glory, as it is written: "A wise son is the glory of his father." (Prov. 10:1) Happy the soul which, tasting the fruit of salvation, is carried along and advances always in the perfume of those ointments so that it may see his glory, the glory as it were of the only-begotten of the Father. Take courage, you who are lost, for to seek and save that which was lost Jesus now comes. Return to health, you who are sick, for with the ointment of his mercy Christ comes to heal all the contrite of heart.

87

Rejoice all you who are ambitious for great things, for the Son of God descends on you to make you co-heirs of his own kingdom. Thus I pray: "Heal me O Lord", and I will be healed; "save me", and I will be saved; "glorify me", and I will be glorified. Then indeed my soul will bless his holy Name, when he will forgive all my iniquities, when he will heal all my infirmities, when he will satisfy my ambitions with good things. It is as if I had already tasted this triple gift of mercy, health, and satisfaction when I hear that Jesus Christ, the Son of God, is born. Otherwise why do we call his name Jesus? Is it not because "he shall save his people from their sins"? (Matt. 1:21) Or why has he willed to be called Christ, the Anointed? Is it not through him that "the yoke shall deteriorate in the presence of the oil"? (Isa. 10:27) Why has the Son of God become man but in order to make all men sons of God? Who, then, will resist his will? Jesus forgives us: who then will condemn us? Christ heals us: who will hurt us? The Son of God raises us up: who will put us down?

Jesus is born: let the person whose sinful conscience deserves eternal damnation rejoice, for Jesus' pity exceeds all crimes, no matter how great their number or enormity. Christ is born: therefore, let the person who is tormented by deeply rooted vices rejoice. For no spiritual illness, no matter how chronic, can stand its ground before Christ's healing ointment. The Son of God is born: let him whose habit it is to desire great things rejoice, for the giver of great things is at hand.

Brothers and sisters, he is the heir: let us receive him reverently, so that his inheritance may be ours. For he who has even given us his own Son, how could he not with him give us all other things? (Rom. 8:32) Let no one disbelieve it; let no one doubt it, for we have a most trustworthy witness: "The Word became flesh and made his dwelling among us." (John 1:14) The Only-Begotten of God resolved to have brothers and sisters, to be the first of many brothers and sisters sharing a common birthright. And in order that the small-mindedness of human frailty should in no way doubt this, he first became a brother to humans; he became the Son of Man; he became a man. So if human beings think this incredible, their own eyes will prevent them from denying it.

"Jesus Christ is born in Bethlehem of Judah." Consider the dignity of this. It is not in the royal city of Jerusalem that he is born, but in Bethlehem, the least among thousands of villages in Judah. O Bethlehem, so very small but forever magnified by him who was so great and who within your walls became so small. Rejoice, Bethlehem, through all your streets let a festive Alleluia be sung. What city, on hearing this news will not envy you for that most precious stable and the glory of that manger? Your name is now celebrated all over the world, and all generations call you blessed. Everywhere, O city of God, glorious things are said of you; everywhere it is sung that "a man is born in her, and the Highest himself has established her." (Ps. 87:5) Everywhere, I repeat, it is preached, everywhere it is proclaimed that "Jesus Christ, the Son of God, is born in Bethlehem of Judah."

Nor is it without good reason that the words "of Judah" are added, which remind us of that promise made to our fathers: "The scepter," it says, "shall not be taken away from Judah, nor a ruler from his thigh, until he who is to be sent has come; and he will be the expectation of nations." (Gen. 49:10) For although salvation comes from the Jews, yet that salvation extends to every corner of the earth. "Judah," it is said, "your brothers will praise you. Your hands will be on the necks of your enemies." (Gen. 49:8) These and other things, which we do not read anywhere that they were accomplished by Judah itself, we see fulfilled in Christ. He is the lion of the tribe of Judah, of whom it is said: "Judah is a lion's whelp; from the prey, my son, you have gone up." (Gen. 49:9) A mighty captor is Christ, who "before the child knows how to call his father or mother, the strength of Damascus and the spoils of Samaria will be taken away."

(Isa. 8:4) A mighty captor is Christ who, ascending on high, led captivity itself captive; not that he derived any benefit for himself; on the contrary, he generously distributed gifts

*The important point for us is that we should learn from all this the manner in which he, who wishes to be born in Bethlehem, wishes to be received.*

to people. These, then, and other similar prophecies, which were spoken of Christ and fulfilled in him, are brought to mind when we hear, "Bethlehem of Judah." Therefore, we have absolutely no need to ask whether anything good can come out of Bethlehem.

The important point for us is that we should learn from all this the manner in which he, who wishes to be born in Bethlehem, wishes to be received. There were perhaps some who thought that a noble palace should be sought in which the King of glory might be gloriously received. But it was not for such glory that he came from his royal throne. "Long life is in her right hand, and in her left hand are riches and glory." (Prov. 3:16) In heaven he possessed an eternal abundance of all these things, but in heaven poverty was not to be found. On earth this commodity of poverty was abundant, excessively so; but people did not recognize its value. It was because of his desire for this commodity that the Son of God came

*. . . think how you also may make of yourself a Bethlehem of Judah, so that he will not despise to be born in you.*

down to take it for himself, and, through his esteem for it, to show us also its value. Adorn, then, O Zion, your bridal couch, but with poverty, with humility. These are the ornaments which please him; and, as Mary can testify, these are the skills in which he likes to be clothed. Sacrifice to your God the abominations of the Egyptians.

Consider lastly that it is in Bethlehem of Judah that he is born. And think how you also may make of yourself a Bethlehem of Judah, so that he will not despise to be born in you. Bethlehem means "the house of bread." Judah means "confession." Therefore if you fill your soul with the food of God's words; if faithfully, though unworthily, and with all the devotion of which you are capable, you receive that Bread which came down from heaven and gives life to the

*Justice in your heart is as
important as bread in your house.*

world, that is, the Body of the Lord Jesus, so that the glorified flesh of the Resurrection may renew and strengthen the old wineskin which is your body, making your body capable to hold the wine in it; if, finally, you live by faith and if you never have to admit with tears that you have forgotten to eat your bread: then you will have become a Bethlehem, worthy indeed to receive the Lord in you.

Only take care also that Judah, "confession," is not lacking. Let Judah, then, be your sanctification, adorning yourself with confession, this being the robe most pleasing to Christ on those who serve him. The Apostle commends this

*Let justice, therefore, be in your heart,
that justice which comes by faith,
for this alone finds glory with God.*

to you very briefly: "With the heart," he says, "we believe and so are justified; and with the mouth we confess and so are saved." (Rom. 10:10) Justice in your heart is as important

91

as bread in your house. Justice is as bread, for "Blessed are they that hunger and thirst after justice; for they shall have their fill." (Matt. 5:6) Let justice, therefore, be in your heart, that justice which comes by faith, for this alone finds glory with God. And in your mouth let there be confession so that you may be saved; thus with confidence may you receive him who is born in Bethlehem of Judah, Jesus Christ the Son of God.

# Jesus, the Very Thought of You

From an extended devotional poem often attributed to Bernard of Clairvaux. This English text is based on a translation by Edward Caswall (1849).

*Jesus, the very thought of you*
*Fills us with sweet delight,*
*But sweeter far your face to view*
*And rest within your light.*

*No voice can sing, no heart can frame,*
*Nor can the memory find*
*A sweeter sound than your blest name,*
*O Savior of mankind!*

*O Hope of every contrite heart,*
*O Joy of all the meek,*
*How kind you are to those who fall,*
*How good to those who seek!*

*But what to those who find? Ah, this*
*No tongue or pen can show;*
*The love of Jesus, what it is*
*None but his loved ones know.*

~ S·E·R·M·O·N ~

# 10

## John Wyclif,
### 1324–1384

*J*ohn Wyclif, a native of Yorkshire, England,
was an Oxford scholar and London priest. He is
known for translating the Scriptures into English
and for preaching the gospel in the people's language,
150 years before the Reformation.

*In this brief three-point sermon, Wyclif expounds the
doctrinal significance of Christ's coming. Christ becomes
human to make satisfaction for sin and Christ's coming
is a testimony to God's righteousness. This objective
doctrinal point is framed by language about our union
with Christ. The sermon begins and ends by naming the
Christmas joy we share because Christ is born in us.*

~ ~

According to the joy that Paul reveals, we may say on Christmas Day that a child is born to us, for Jesus Christ, we believe, is born on this day. And in this sense God spoke, both in figure and in letter, that a child is born to us, a child in whom we should have this joy. And three short words are to be spoken from Isaiah's speech so that people may afterward rejoice in serving this child.

First, we believe that because our first elders sinned there must be satisfaction made by the righteousness of God. For as God is merciful, so is he full of righteousness. But how should he judge the whole world unless he kept righteousness in it? For the Lord against whom this sin was done is God Almighty; and no sin may be done except against God. And the greater the Lord is against whom the sin is done, the more is that sin to be punished by this Lord. It would be a great sin to act against the king's commands; but to act against God's commands is even more inexcusable.

We believe that God told Adam not to eat the apple. But he broke God's command, and he was not excused for that sin, neither by his own folly (or weakness), nor by Eve, nor by the serpent. And so by the righteousness of God this sin must always be punished. And it lacks discernment to say that God might by his power forgive this sin without the satisfaction that was made for it. For God has the power to do this, but his justice will not permit anything else except that each sin be punished, either on earth or in hell. And God may not accept a person and forget his sin without satisfaction, else he must give humans and angels free permission to sin. And this is the first lesson that we take from our faith.

The second teaching that we take is that he who should make satisfaction for the sin of our first father must be both God and human. For since humanity sinned, humanity must make satisfaction. And therefore an angel could not make satisfaction for humans, for an angel does not have the right and it was not his nature that sinned. But since all humans are one humanity, humanity makes satisfaction for humans if any member of humanity makes satisfaction for all humans.

And in this way we see that if God made another human who was after the nature of Adam, that person would be accountable to God for himself and so could not make satisfaction for himself and for Adam's sin. And since satisfaction had to be made also for Adam's sin, as it is said, such

> *. . . if we truly desire that this Child be born to us, we take joy in this Child and we follow him in three virtues: in righteousness, and meekness, and patience for our God.*

a person who makes the satisfaction must be both God and human; for the worthiness of this person's deeds must be equal to the unworthiness of the sin.

The third teaching that must follow these two is that a Child is born to humans to make satisfaction for human sin. And this Child needs to be God and human given to humanity. And he must bear his empire upon his shoulder, and suffer for humanity. And this Child is Jesus Christ who we presume was born today. And we presume that this Child is born only to those who follow his way of living, for he was born against the others. Those who are unjust and proud and rebel against God are judged by Christ and must be condemned by him; and if they are unkind against his Spirit, they are always condemned to death.

And thus, if we truly desire that this Child be born to us, we take joy in this Child and we follow him in three virtues: in righteousness, and meekness, and patience for our God. For whoever, against the Spirit, condemns Christ unto his death, will be condemned by this Child, even as all others will be saved. And thus the joy of this Child who was meek and full of virtues should make people have little malice so that they then observe the feast well.

To them that will fight and criticize, I say, that this Child who is born is Prince of Peace and loves peace; he condemns contrary people who are contrary to peace. For we study

> *. . . this Child who is born is Prince of Peace*
> *and loves peace . . .*

how Christ came in the fullness of time when he should, and how he came in meekness, as his birth teaches us, and how he came in patience from his birth to his death—and we follow him in these three because of the joy that we have in him. For this joy, in this patience of Christ, brings us to a joy that shall last forever.

# COME AND STAND AMAZED

A medieval Dutch carol, based on a translation by Klaas Hart (1906–1973).

*Come and stand amazed, you people,*
*See how God is reconciled!*
*See his plans of love accomplished,*
*See his gift, this newborn child.*
*See the Mighty, weak and tender,*
*See the Word who now is mute.*
*See the Sovereign without splendor,*
*See the Fullness destitute;*
*The Beloved, whom we covet,*
*In a state of low repute.*

*See how humankind received him;*
*See him wrapped in swaddling bands,*
*Who as Lord of all creation*
*Rules the wind by his commands.*
*See him lying in a manger*
*Without sign of reasoning;*
*Word of God to flesh surrendered,*
*He is wisdom's crown, our King.*
*See how tender our Defender*
*At whose birth the angels sing.*

*O Lord Jesus, God incarnate,*
*Who assumed this humble form,*
*Counsel me and let my wishes*
*To your perfect will conform.*
*Light of life, dispel my darkness,*
*Let your frailty strengthen me;*
*Let your meekness give me boldness,*
*Let your burden set me free;*
*Let your sadness give me gladness,*
*Let your death be life for me.*

# O LOVE HOW DEEP, HOW BROAD, HOW HIGH

From a fifteenth-century manuscript, a text often attributed to Thomas à Kempis. This English text is based on a translation by Benjamin Webb (1854).

*O love, how deep, how broad, how high,*
*Beyond all thought and fantasy,*
*That God, the Son of God, should take*
*Our mortal form for mortals' sake!*

*For us baptized, for us he bore*
*His holy fast and hungered sore;*
*For us temptation sharp he knew,*
*For us the tempter overthrew.*

*For us he prayed; for us he taught;*
*For us his daily works he wrought:*
*By words and signs and actions thus*
*Still seeking not himself, but us.*

*For us to evil power betrayed,*
*Scourged, mocked, in purple robe arrayed,*
*He bore the shameful cross and death;*
*For us gave up his dying breath.*

*For us he rose from death again;*
*For us he went on high to reign;*
*For us he sent his Spirit here*
*To guide, to strengthen, and to cheer.*

*All glory to our Lord and God*
*For love so deep, so high, so broad—*
*The Trinity, whom we adore*
*Forever and forevermore.*

# 11

## Thomas à Kempis,
### 1380—1471

*T*homas à Kempis was born in a small town in
the Rhine Valley and was schooled in what is now
the Netherlands. He was part of a religious renewal
movement, the Devotio Moderna, that fostered a deep
piety among ordinary Christians. He is best known as the
author of the devotional classic The Imitation of Christ.

If Leo's sermon reads like a creed, Thomas' reads like
a poetic prayer, beginning as a summons to receive Christ
and building to a grand doxology of the Trinity. As with
Leo, the sermon features the liturgical "time warp" of
placing ourselves at the events we celebrate. The sermon is
marked by an intense immediacy, a sense that the present
moment is charged with significance because of Christ's
present coming.

⤙ ⤚

"Seek the Lord, while he may be found; call on him, while he is near." (Isa. 55:6) Arise, all you faithful of Christ: eagerly gather for this reverent observance of the Lord's birth. For this is the most holy night on which the Redeemer of the world, Jesus Christ, chose to be born of the glorious Virgin Mary. Arise, therefore, all, and watch. Prepare your hearts and pray. The Lord has come. Come and adore. Seek Jesus, and you will find him. Knock at the door, and it will be opened to you. Enter the house and you will see. Our King has arrived. Christ has been born to us. Come, let us adore and fall down before him: for he it is who made us. Come, you angels and archangels: chant and rejoice and sing psalms. Be glad, you just in the Lord: sing a hymn to our God. Proclaim his works among the nations. God has

*Arise, all you faithful of Christ: eagerly gather for this reverent observance of the Lord's birth.*

come in the flesh. He who is never away from us in the divine is with us in human nature. Come, little and great, old and aged, youths and maidens: sing to the Lord a new song, for he has done wonders this day. Lift up your hearts with your hands to heaven, and above all rejoicing give glory to his praise.

The Lord is with us: do not be sad. Put on the garments of gladness and joy, you chosen ones of God. Cast away the

*The Lord is with us: do not be sad.*

works of darkness, and put on the armor of light. As in the light of day, so let us watch this sacred night. Let us rejoice and exult. Let us sing songs and hymns. Let us praise God our Savior. Let us offer him our vows. Let us present him the service of our mouth. The Lord is with us, depart not, weary not, but stand strongly, and sing psalms to him with cheerfulness.

Who can sleep now, while the angels are singing in the heavens and the voice of praise resounds on high? Who would remain in bed, while all rejoice to be with Jesus in gladness? Who would not eagerly rise this night, when all things seem to be rejoicing?

Therefore be glad and rejoice, daughter of Zion; give praise, O Jerusalem. For this day true peace has come down from heaven, to appease and restore the things that are in

*Who can sleep now, while the angels are singing in the heavens and the voice of praise resounds on high?*

heaven and the things that are on earth. This day the true Light has shone on the earth, to enlighten everyone that believes in him. This day there is great joy in Israel, for Christ is born in Bethlehem. This day throughout the world the heavens are flowing with honey; for from the mouth of the learned comes very sweet speeches by which the weak are refreshed, the devout consoled, the ignorant instructed, the slothful aroused, the faithful strengthened, and unbelievers put to shame.

Today the angels rejoice, the archangels exult, and all the just are expressing adoration and spiritual joy. Today night is turned into day and great brightness, for to those with righteous hearts a light has risen up in darkness, the merciful and compassionate Lord. Let this night be blessed forever and numbered among the days of reverent observance. Let them bless it who are accustomed to blessing the day; and praise it all the children of light, for on this day is born Christ the Son of God, the Light of eternal light. Let it not be dark, but let it be illumined by a light from above; and throughout the whole Church let many lamps be lighted. Let nothing on this day be passed over that concerns its beauty, but let its praise be continued even to the breaking of the rising dawn. And when the day shall have dawned, may the Sun of Justice, who is born, shine in the hearts of all those who love him, and may fresh devotion again rise in the hearts of all who celebrate. A holy day has shone upon us today. Let all the faithful rejoice: for God gave a sign long ago, saying, "Let there be light," and light was made.

O truly blessed night, brightened by the birth of the true Light, and made resplendent with the glory of angels, by whose hymns and praises it is rendered even more joyful for all the faithful throughout the world.

O truly most blessed night, more brilliant than all the nights of time, which was privileged to know the season

*Blessed therefore be the holy Trinity,*
*by whose goodness and wisdom the*
*dignity of humanity has been restored*
*and the cunning of the devil deceived.*

and the hour when the Son of God came from the virgin's womb, clothed in the body of our weakness.

O sacred and stainless nativity, which the fruitfulness of a virgin delivered.

O fruitfulness above nature, which the purity of a virgin beautified, and the sovereign majesty chose in order that mortal human beings might be saved.

O blessed and joyful birth, which has changed the curse of our first parents into blessing and has turned their grief into everlasting joy. This night is truly worthy of the awe and love of all people, the night in which Christ permitted himself to be delivered in order to deliver all.

Blessed therefore be the holy Trinity, by whose goodness and wisdom the dignity of humanity has been restored and the cunning of the devil deceived. I bless you, heavenly Father, who sent your beloved Son into the world for our redemption. I bless you only-begotten Son of God, Jesus Christ, who to redeem us assumed our nature. I bless you,

*To you be infinite praise and glory, to you be honor and empire, O supreme, eternal Trinity, by whose providence and ordering so sweet and solemn a festival has come to us.*

Holy Spirit, the paraclete, who gloriously and wondrously perfected all the mysteries of our redemption from the beginning to the end. To you be infinite praise and glory, to you be honor and empire, O supreme, eternal Trinity, by whose providence and ordering so sweet and solemn a festival has come to us. Amen.

# IN DULCI JUBILO

A fourteenth-century German carol, originally set in both Latin and German, later known through the free paraphrase "Good Christian Friends, Rejoice."

In dulci jubilo *[In sweet rejoicing]*
*Now sing with hearts aglow!*
*Our delight and pleasure*
*Lies* in praesepio, *[in a manger]*
*Like sunshine is our treasure*
Matris in gremio. *[on the lap of the mother]*
Alpha es et O! *[You are beginning and end]*

O Jesu, parvule, *[O infant Jesus]*
*For thee I long alway;*
*Comfort my heart's blindness,*
O puer optime, *[O best of boys]*
*With all thy loving-kindness,*
O princeps gloriae. *[O Prince of glory]*
Trahe me post te! *[Draw me after you]*

O Patris caritas! *[O love of the Father]*
O Nati lenitas! *[O mercy of the Son]*
*Deeply were we stainèd*
Per nostra crimina; *[through our sins]*
*But thou for us hast gainèd*
Coelorum gaudia. *[the joys of heaven]*
*O that we were there!*

Ubi sunt gaudia *[Where are joys]*
*In any place but there?*
*There are angels singing*
Nova cantica, *[new songs]*
*And there the bells are ringing*
In Regis curia. *[in the court of the King]*
*O that we were there!*

106

# 12

# Martin Luther,
## 1483–1546

*M artin Luther is widely known as a church
reformer and astute biblical scholar. But
none of his contributions can be fully
understood without taking into account his
preaching, for it was in his preaching that both his biblical
acumen and pastoral concern meet. It was in his preaching
that his ideas were expressed in ways that motivated both
ordinary citizens and civic rulers to consider the cause of
reforming the church. Luther preached somewhere around
5,000 sermons during his life.*

*This text is but one of over sixty sermons on Luke 2 and
John 1 that Luther preached on Christmas. Throughout
this sermon, Luther is intensely personal. He challenges
listeners not merely to recall that Jesus "is the Lord and
Savior," but also to accept the fact that he is "your Lord*

*and Savior." In this way, this sermon is one of the most*
*evangelistic sermons in this volume. Fittingly, the sermon*
*culminates in a popular German carol about the delight*
*that worshipers experience in discovering that the babe*
*born in a manger came for them.*

⌒ ⌐

For whom was he born and whose Lord and Savior is he?
The angels declare that he was born Lord and Savior. The
Turks, the pope, and the scholars say the same thing, but
only to the extent that it brings in money and honor. But
that anyone could say, "to *you* is born," as the angel says,
this is the faith which we must preach about. But we cannot
preach about it as we would like to do. Indeed, who could
ever grasp the full meaning of these words of the evangelist:
"a Savior, who is the Lord," and, "to you"! I know well
enough how to talk about it and what to believe about it,
just as others do. So there are many who have this belief
and do not doubt this first belief that Christ is the Lord, the
Savior, and the virgin's Son. This I too have never doubted.
But if these words are planted no higher than in my thoughts,
then they have no firm roots. We are certain that this was

> *Beyond the first faith there must be*
> *the second faith, that Christ is not only*
> *the virgin's Son, but also the Lord of angels*
> *and the Savior of humanity.*

proclaimed by the angel, but the firm faith does not follow.
For the reason does not understand both sides of this faith,
first that Christ is a man, but also the Savior and Lord or
King. This needs to be revealed from heaven. One who really
has the first faith also has the other.

Who, then, are those to whom this joyful news is to be proclaimed? Those who are faint-hearted and feel the burden of their sins, like the shepherds to whom the angels proclaim the message; letting the great lords in Jerusalem, who do not accept it, go on sleeping. Beyond the first faith there must be the second faith, that Christ is not only the virgin's Son, but also the Lord of angels and the Savior of humanity. Anyone can understand the words—antisacramentarians, fanatics, sectarians, and Turks; but they do not proceed from the heart, they come only from hearing and go no farther than hearing. This is not faith, however, but only a memory of what has been heard, that one knows that one has heard it. Nobody gambles on it, so as to stake goods, life, and honor on it. And yet we must preach it for the sake of those who are in the crowd to whom the angel preached.

This is our theology, which we preach in order that we may understand what the angel wants. Mary gave birth to the child, took it to her breast and nursed it, and the Father in heaven has his Son lying in the manger and the mother's lap. Why did God do all this? Why does Mary guard the child as a mother should? And reason answers: in order that we may make an idol of her, that honor may be paid to the mother. Mary becomes all this without her knowledge and consent, and all the songs and glory and honor are addressed to the mother. And yet the text does not proclaim the honor of the mother, for the angel says, "I bring you good news of great joy; for to you the Savior is born today." (Luke 2:10–11) I am to accept the child and his birth and forget the mother, as far as this is possible, although her part cannot be forgotten, for where there is a birth there must also be a mother. Nevertheless, we dare not put our faith in the mother but only in the fact that the child was born. And the angel desired that we should see nothing but the child which is born, just as the angels themselves, as though they were blind, saw nothing but the child born of the virgin, and desired that all created things should be as nothing compared with this child, that we should see nothing, be it harps, gold, goods, honor, power, and the like, which we would prefer before their message. For if I receive even the costliest and best in the world, it still does not have the name of Savior. And if the Turk were ten times stronger than he is, he could not for one moment save me from my infirmity, to say nothing of the peril of death, and even less from the smallest sin or from death itself. In my sin, my death, I must depart all created things. No; sun, moon, stars, all creatures, physicians, emperors, kings, wise persons, and lords cannot help me. When I die I will see nothing but black darkness, and yet that light, "to you the Savior is born today," (Luke 2:11) remains in my eyes and fills all heaven and earth. The Savior will help me when all have forsaken me. And when the heavens and the stars and all creatures stare at me with horrible expression, I see nothing in heaven and earth but this child. So great should that light which declares that he is my Savior become in my eyes that I can say: "Mary, you did not bear this child for yourself alone. The child is not yours; you did not bear him for yourself, but for me, even though you are his mother, even though you held him in your arms and wrapped him in swaddling clothes and picked him up and laid him down. But I have a greater honor than your honor as his mother. For your honor pertains to your motherhood of the body of the child, but my honor is this, that you have my treasure, so that I know none, neither human nor angels, who can help me except this child whom you, O Mary, hold in your arms. If a person could put out of his mind all that he is and has except this child, and if for him everything—money, goods, power, or honor—fades into darkness and he despises everything on earth compared with this child, so that heaven with its stars and earth with all its power and all its treasures becomes as nothing to him, that person would have the true benefit and fruit of this message of the angel. And for us the time must come when suddenly all will be darkness and we will know nothing but this message of the angel: "I bring you good news of great joy; for to you the Savior is born today." (Luke 2:10–11)

This, then, is the faith we preach, of which the Turks and the pope and all the sectarians know nothing. The fanatics do, it is true, snatch to themselves the words of the angels, but how sincere they are is plain to see. For they receive the Word only as a piece of paper, as the cup and corporal receive the body and blood of Christ. The paper does no

> *. . . O human, . . . not only learn that Christ, born of the virgin, is the Lord and Savior, but also accept the fact that he is your Lord and Savior . . .*

more than contain something and pass it on to others, but yet it remains paper. Thus you copy something from one paper on another paper. From my tongue the Word sounds in your ear, but it does not go to the heart. So they receive this greatest of treasures to their great harm and still think they are Christians, just as though the paper were to say: I certainly have in me the written words, "to you the Savior is born today"; therefore I will be saved. But then the fire comes and burns up the paper.

Therefore this is the chief article which separates us from all the heathen, that you, O human, may not only learn that Christ, born of the virgin, is the Lord and Savior, but also accept the fact that he is your Lord and Savior, that you may be able to boast in your heart, "I hear the Word that sounds from heaven and says, 'This child who is born of the virgin is not only his mother's son.' I have more than the mother's estate. He is more mine than Mary's, for he was born for me, for the angel said, 'To you' the Savior is born." Then you ought to say, "Amen, I thank you, dear Lord."

But then reason says: Who knows? I believe that Christ, born of the virgin, is the Lord and Savior and he may perhaps help Peter and Paul, but he was not born for me, a sinner. But even if you believed that much, it would still not be enough, unless there were added to it the faith that he was born for you. For he was not born merely in order that I should honor the mother, that she should be praised because he was born of the virgin mother. This honor belongs to none except her and it is not to be despised, for the angel said, "Blessed are you among women!" (Luke 1:28) But it must not be too highly honored so that one may not deny what is written here: "To you the Savior is born today."

*Examine yourself and see whether you are a Christian! If you can sing: "The Son, who is proclaimed to be a Lord and Savior, is my Savior"; and if you can confirm the message of the angel and say yes to it and believe it in your heart, then your heart will be filled with assurance and joy and confidence, and you will not worry about even the costliest and best that this world has to offer.*

He was not merely concerned to be born of a virgin; it was infinitely more than that. It was this, as she herself sings in the Magnificat: "He has helped his servant Israel"; (Luke 1:54) not that he was born of me and my virginity, but born for you and for your benefit, not only for my honor.

Examine yourself and see whether you are a Christian! If you can sing: "The Son, who is proclaimed to be a Lord and Savior, is my Savior"; and if you can confirm the message of the angel and say yes to it and believe it in your heart, then your heart will be filled with assurance and joy and confidence, and you will not worry about even the costliest and best that this world has to offer. For when I speak to the virgin from the bottom of my heart and say: "O Mary, noble, tender virgin, you have given birth to a child; this I want more than robes and guldens, yes, more than my body and life," then you are closer to the treasure than everything else in heaven and earth. As Psalm 73[:25] says, "There is nothing on earth that I desire besides you." You see how a person rejoices when receiving a robe or ten guldens. But how many are there who shout and jump for joy when they hear the message of the angel: "To you the Savior is born today"? Indeed, the majority look upon it as a sermon that must be preached, and when they have heard it, consider it a trifling thing, and go away just as they were before. This shows that we have neither the first nor the second faith. We do not believe that the virgin mother gave birth to a son and that he is the Lord and Savior unless, added to this, I believe the second thing, namely, that he is my Savior and Lord. When I can say, "This I accept as my own, because the angel meant it for me, then, if I believe it in my heart, I will not fail to love the mother Mary, and even more the child, and especially the Father. For, if it is true that the child was born of the virgin and is mine, then I have no angry God and I must know and feel that there is nothing but laughter and joy in the heart of the Father and no sadness in my heart. For, if what the angel says is true, that he is our Lord and Savior, what can sin do against us? "If God is for us, who is against us?" (Rom. 8:31) I cannot speak greater words than these, nor can all the angels and even the Holy Spirit, as is sufficiently testified by the beautiful and devout songs that have been made about it. I do not trust myself to express it. I most gladly hear you sing and speak of it, but as long as no joy is there, so long is faith still weak or even non-existent, and you still do not believe the angel.

You can see what our papists and Junkers, who have chosen countless saviors, have felt about this faith. Indeed, the papists still want to retain the mass, the invocation of saints, and their invented works by which we are to be saved.

This is as much as to say, "I do not believe in the Savior and Lord whom Mary bore." And yet they sing the words of the angel, hold their triple masses [at Christmas] and play their organs. They speak the words with their tongues but their heart has another savior. And the same is true in the monasteries: if you want to be saved, remember to keep the rule and regulations of Francis [the monastic regulations associated with St. Francis of Assisi] and you will have a gracious God! And at the Diet of Augsburg they decided to stick to this. In the name of all the devils, let them stick there! It has been said sufficiently that this Savior lies in the manger. But if there is any other thing that saves me, then I rightly call it my savior. If the sun, moon, and stars save, I can call them saviors. If St. Bartholomew or St. Anthony or a pilgrimage to St. James or good works save, then surely they are my savior. If St. Francis, then he is my savior. But then what is left of the honor of the child who was born this day, whom the angel calls Lord and Savior, and who wants to keep his name, which is Savior and Christ the Lord. If I set up any savior except this child, no matter who or what it is or is called, then he is not the Savior. But the text says that he is the Savior. And if this is true—and it is the truth—then let everything else go.

One who hears the message of the angel and believes it will be filled with fear, like the shepherds. True, it is too lofty for me to believe that I should come to this treasure without any merit on my part. And yet, it must be so. In the papacy this message was not preached in the pulpit, and I am afraid that it will disappear again. It was the other message that the devil initiated and has allowed to remain in the papacy. All their hymns are to this effect. Among the Turks the devil has completely wiped it out. Therefore, remember it, sing it, and learn it, while there is still time! I fear that the time will come when we shall not be allowed to hear, believe, and sing this message in public, and the time has already come when it is no longer understood; though Satan does allow it to be spoken with the mouth, as the papists do. But when it comes to declaring that he is born for you, and to singing:

> *In dulci jubilo*
> Now sing with hearts aglow!
>   Our delight and pleasure
> Lies *in praesepio,*
>   Like sunshine is our treasure
> *Matris in gremio*
> *Alpha est et O!*

this he is unwilling to allow.

What we have said, then, has been about that second faith, which is not only to believe in Mary's Son, but rather that he who lies in the virgin's lap is our Savior, that you accept this and give thanks to God, who so loved you that he gave you a Savior who is yours. And for a sign he sent the angel from heaven to proclaim him, in order that nothing else should be preached except that this child is the Savior and far better than heaven and earth. Him, therefore, we should acknowledge and accept; confess him as our Savior in every need, call upon him, and never doubt that he will save us from all misfortune. Amen.

# FROM HEAVEN ABOVE

Written by Martin Luther for his family's Christmas devotions and first published in 1535. This English text is a translation by Roland Bainton.

### An Angel
*From heaven high I come to earth.*
*I bring you tidings of great mirth.*
*This mirth is such a wondrous thing*
*That I must tell you all and sing.*

*A little child for you this morn*
*Has from a chosen maid been born,*
*A little child so tender, sweet,*
*That you should skip upon your feet.*

*He is the Christ, our God indeed,*
*Who saves you all in every need.*
*He will himself your Savior be.*
*From all wrong doing make you free.*

*He brings you every one to bliss.*
*The heavenly Father sees to this.*
*You shall be here with us on high.*
*Here shall you live and never die.*

*Look now, you children, at the sign,*
*A manger cradle far from fine.*
*A tiny baby you will see.*
*Upholder of the world is he.*

### Children
*How glad we'll be if it is so!*
*With all the shepherds let us go*
*To see what God for us has done*
*In sending us his own dear Son.*

*Look, look, my heart, and let me peek.*
*Whom in the manger do you seek?*

*Who is that lovely little one?*
*The Baby Jesus, God's own Son.*

*Be welcome, Lord; be now our guest.*
*By you poor sinners have been blessed.*
*In nakedness and cold you lie.*
*How can I thank you—how can I?*

*O Lord, who made and molded all,*
*How did you come to be so small*
*That you should lie upon dry grass,*
*The fodder of the ox and ass?*

*And if the world were twice as wide,*
*With gold and precious jewels inside,*
*Still such a cradle would not do*
*To hold a babe as great as you.*

*The velvet and the silken ruff,*
*For these the hay is good enough.*
*Here lies a prince and Lord of all,*
*A king within an ass's stall.*

*You wanted so to make me know*
*That you had let all great things go.*
*You had a palace in the sky;*
*You left it there for such as I.*

*O dear Lord Jesus, for your head*
*Now will I make the softest bed.*
*The chamber where this bed shall be*
*Is in my heart, inside of me.*

*I can play the whole day long.*
*I'll dance and sing for you a song,*
*A soft and soothing lullaby,*
*So sweet that you will never cry.*

**All**
*To God who sent his only Son,*
*Be glory, laud and honor done.*
*Let all the choir of heaven rejoice,*
*The new ring in with heart and voice.*

~ S E R M O N ~

# 13

## John Calvin,
## 1509–1564

*J*ohn Calvin was trained as a lawyer and
a humanist and provided some of the most
mature theological statements of the Reformation
period. During his extended ministry in Geneva, as
well as a brief sojourn in Strasbourg, he preached several
times a week, mostly in extended series of sermons on
particular biblical books.

Although Calvin preached with little regard to the
church year, he did naturally preach several of his sermons
on events in Jesus' life as recorded in the Gospels. This
sermon on the nativity is developed around a pastoral
concern to assure believers of their security as God's
children. It features striking rhetorical flourishes ("He
willed to be not only a mortal man clothed in our nature,
but, as it were, a poor earthworm stripped of all good"),

*particularly concerned with drawing contrasts between humanity's lowliness and divine grandeur. The sermon features extended reflections on several aspects of the Christmas story (the shepherds, the song of the angels, the magi, the city of Bethlehem) before culminating in an invitation to the Lord's Table. Many paragraphs drive toward the pastoral purpose of a given aspect of Christian doctrine, pointing out how Christ's coming is a source of comfort, confidence, encouragement, learning, and challenge.*

We know that it is our good, our joy and repose to be united with the Son of God. Since he is our Head, we are his body, and we also receive from him our life and our salvation and all good. In fact, we know that our condition would be miserable if we did not have our refuge in him and were not kept in his care. We could not reach so high (given that we can barely crawl on the earth) unless he approached us from his side and already had approached in his birth, when he clothed himself in our flesh and made himself our brother. We could not now have our refuge in our Lord Jesus Christ's being seated at the right hand of God his Father in heavenly glory, unless he were brought down to the extent of being made a mortal human and having a

> *Let us recognize also how our Lord Jesus Christ, ever since his birth, suffered for us so that when we seek him we do not need to make long journeys to find him nor to be truly united to him.*

condition in common with us. That is also why, when he is called "Mediator between God and humans," this title

120

"human" is especially attributed to him. And for the same reason he is called "Emmanuel," that is, "God with us."

Yet when we seek our Lord Jesus Christ in order to find in him relief from all our miseries and a sure and reliable protection, we must begin at his birth. Not only are we told that he was made human like us, but that he emptied himself in such a way that he was barely thought to be of the rank of humans. He was, as it were, banished from every house and fellowship. There was nothing except a stable and a manger to receive him.

Therefore, we know how God displayed the infinite treasures of his goodness when he willed that his Son might be humbled in this way for our sakes. Let us recognize also how our Lord Jesus Christ, ever since his birth, suffered for us so that when we seek him we do not need to make long journeys to find him nor to be truly united to him. For this reason he willed to be subject to every shame, in such a way that he was, as it were, rejected by the rest of humanity.

But let us also learn to be little in order to be received by him. For it is at least reasonable that there is conformity between the Head and the members. Humans do not need to empty themselves in order to be of no value. For already

*Even though he took our condition, he was able to maintain his heavenly majesty.*

by nature they will find such poverty in themselves that they will have good reason to be thoroughly dejected. But let us know what we are like so that we may offer ourselves to our Lord Jesus Christ in true humility—and so that he may recognize us and acknowledge us as his own.

However, we also have to note that, in the history which St. Luke narrates, on the one hand we learn how the Son of God emptied himself of everything for our salvation. On the other hand, we also learn that he left certain and infallible testimony that he was the Redeemer of the world who was always promised. Even though he took our condition, he was able to maintain his heavenly majesty. Both sides are shown to us here. For our Lord Jesus Christ is here in a manger and he is, as it were, rejected by the world. He is in extreme poverty without any honor, without any reputation, as if subjected to being a servant. Yet he is praised and honored by angels from Paradise. In the first place, an angel brings the message of his birth. Then the same angel is accompanied by a great multitude, even by an army, who are all present and appear as witnesses sent by God to show that our Lord Jesus Christ, being so humbled for the salvation of humanity, never stops being King of all the world and having everything under his dominion.

The place, Bethlehem, also gives proof that it was he who had always been promised. For the prophet Micah had said: "And you Bethlehem, though you are in great contempt, as a village which is not much to look at and which is not densely populated, yet from you will come for me the one who is to govern my people, and his origin will be from all eternity." (cf. Micah 5:2)

We see, then, on the one hand how our Lord Jesus Christ did not spare himself, so that we might have easy access to him and that we might not doubt that we are received even as his body, since he willed to be not only a mortal man clothed in our nature, but, as it were, a poor earthworm stripped of all good. May we never doubt, then, however miserable we may be, that he will keep us as his members.

On the other hand, we see him marked, as it were, by the hand of God, so that he may be received without any difficulty, as him from whom we must expect salvation and by whom we are received into the Kingdom of God from which we were previously banished. For we see that he has in himself a divine majesty, since the angels recognize him as their superior and their sovereign King. We should not doubt, when we are under his care, that he has all that is

needed to provide for us. Let us know, however much he
was humbled, it in no way takes away from his divine power
nor hinders us from being securely under his guidance.

Now we see the summary of this history: first, we know
that the Son of God, even our Mediator, has united himself
to us in such a way that we must never doubt that we are
sharers both of his life and of all his riches. Let us also know
that he brought with himself everything that was required
for our salvation. For (as I have already said) he was not
emptied in such a way that he was ever without his divine
majesty. Although before humans he had no reputation, yet
he always remained not only heir of this world (since he is
the head of the Church), but also always true God.

## The Shepherds and Magi

Besides, let us learn from those who are here ordained
as teachers and leaders how we must come to our Lord
Jesus Christ. Certainly the wise people of this world are so
inflated with pride and presumption that they will scarcely
humble themselves to be scholars of unlearned people and
poor shepherds from the fields. But it is all our wisdom that
we learn from these shepherds (of whom Luke speaks) to
come to our Lord Jesus Christ. For although we may have
all the sciences of the world stuffed into our heads, of what

> *For although we may have all the sciences
> of the world stuffed into our heads,
> of what use will it be when life fails us?*

use will it be when life fails us? How will it help us to know
"him in whom the treasures of all wisdom are hidden," as
St. Paul says? Now we see where we must begin. It does
us no harm to follow those who have shown us the way to
come to our Lord Jesus Christ.

God gave this honor neither to the great people of this world, nor to the wise, nor to the rich, nor to the nobles, but he chose shepherds. Therefore, let us follow that order. It is true that wisemen came from the East to honor our Lord Jesus Christ. But the shepherds had to come first, in order that all presumption might be destroyed and that those who would be regarded as Christians must be as fools in this world. So, let us not bring a foolish presumption to judge by our imaginations the admirable secrets of God, but let us adore them in all simplicity.

Further, let us look at the faith which was in these shepherds. Then it will no longer be difficult to follow them. They come to adore the Redeemer of the world. And in what condition do they find him? There he is laid in a manger and wrapped in a few little cloths, and it is the sign which had been given to them by the angel. Now it surely seemed that this was to astonish them and even to make them turn their backs in such a manner that they might no longer recognize Jesus Christ as their Savior.

*So, let us not bring a foolish presumption to judge by our imaginations the admirable secrets of God, but let us adore them in all simplicity.*

For the Scribes and Teachers of the Jews surely thought that the Redeemer who had been promised must come with an extravagant display. Moreover, they thought that he must subject all the world in such a way that he would have only prosperity, that they would get abundant wealth to glut themselves, and that they would gather all the riches of the world. Here, then, was a scandal which could make these poor people lose courage, so that they would never have come to our Lord Jesus Christ but would have been entirely alienated from him, when it is said to them that they will find him in a stable and wrapped with rags. The sign given to them of the Redeemer is that he will be laid in a manger as if he were cut off from the rank of humans. Yet even that does not turn them away. So they come to know him as Lord, confessing how God has had pity on them and that finally he willed to fulfill his promise which he had always given, and they are assured by such a sight.

Since, then, the faith of these shepherds was so great that it fought against everything that could turn them from coming to our Lord Jesus Christ, we shall be doubly guilty and stripped of every excuse, unless we learn in their school, unless the birth of our Lord Jesus Christ (although he appeared without this world's dignity or extravagant display or nobility) is not a scandal to hinder us or to make us turn away from the good way, unless we come to surrender to him as our sovereign King to whom all dominion is given in heaven and on earth. In fact, we need such a warning. For, as I have already mentioned, the doctrine of the Gospel brings only scandal to those who are preoccupied with pride and folly and who assume that they are wise.

We see also how many fanatics reject everything which is contrary to their brains. There are, on the other hand, many mockers who have never been touched by any feeling of their sins. Because they are worldly people who think they will

> *This, then, is how we must practice*
> *this teaching: we must come to our*
> *Lord Jesus Christ even though, at first sight,*
> *we do not find in him what our flesh,*
> *that is, our natural senses, desire.*

never be held accountable and who do not know whether there is a better life than the one they see here below, they judge that it is only foolishness to follow the Son of God and to acquaint oneself with him. Let us see, then, how much more we should be strengthened by this warning that the Son of God does not lose any of his majesty and glory, and that it is not decreased in his humiliation for our salvation: we should be thrilled by this, knowing his immeasurable goodness and the love he has shown us.

This, then, is how we must practice this teaching: we must come to our Lord Jesus Christ even though, at first sight, we do not find in him what our flesh, that is, our natural senses, desire. Although he was wrapped in rags at his birth and although he had been laid there in the manger, may we know and be resolved that he did not cease to be Mediator to draw us to God his Father, to give us an entrance into the Kingdom of heaven from which we were completely shut out. Even more so today, although he does not rule with extravagant display and although his Church is despised and although there is a simplicity in his Word which the great people of this world reject, as for us, may we never for these reasons stop clinging to him and subjecting ourselves to his rule in a true obedience of faith. For example, when one preaches, it is not something which attracts us much in our tradition. We hear a man speaking. And who is he? He is not of great dignity and reputation. So, in sum, there is only the word. On the other hand, in what is preached by

*So let us know we cannot draw near*
*to what God shows and declares to us,*
*unless we have first bowed down.*

the Gospel there are many things which seem to us to be against all reason, when we wish to judge them according to our taste. So let us know we cannot draw near to what God shows and declares to us, unless we have first bowed down.

For our sakes he adds the sacraments to his Word as a confirmation. And would a drop of water be sufficient to assure us of the forgiveness of our sin and that God adopted us as his children and, though we are feeble and frail, that we will be clothed with his heavenly glory which will never fail us? Could we find a guarantee and assurance of things so great and so excellent in a little water? In the Holy Supper would a piece of bread and a drop of wine be sufficient to assure us that God accepts us as his children, that we live in Jesus Christ, and that he has shared everything with us? For it seems that such ceremonies which have no extravagant display can have no value. So then, we see even better how what is here mentioned about the shepherds applies to us and how we should benefit from it today. In other words, let us not stop drawing near to our Lord Jesus Christ and being assured that it is he in whom we will find all good, all rejoicing, and all glory, although it seems that he is still, as it were, in the stable and in the manger, wrapped with swaddling clothes. There might be many things which could corrupt us and dazzle the eyes of a few so that they might not perceive the heavenly glory which was given to him by God his Father, I mean, even in the human nature he took from us. For since he is God, he has everything from himself (as it is said in the seventeenth chapter of St. John), but with respect to his humanity he received as a free gift everything that he brought to us, that we might draw from his fullness, and that we might find in him everything that is desirable, and that we might have all our repose and contentment in him alone.

In addition, let us note well that the Holy Spirit also wished to assure us that by following the shepherds who are here ordained as teachers and guides, we should have no fear of making a mistake. For if the shepherds had no other sign than the stable and the manger, we could say, "Look at the poor idiots who make themselves believe foolishly and without reason that he was the Redeemer of the world." That would be entirely too easy for us. We could, then, be in doubt. But the shepherds were confirmed in other ways to be certain that he who was laid in the manger was the Son of God. When the angel appeared to them, then they heard this song, which St. Luke adds, in which all the Kingdom of heaven testifies to our Lord Jesus Christ, that he has all power over creatures in heaven and on earth.

Let us learn, then, to receive (to be assured in the faith of Jesus Christ) everything offered to us here. For it is certain that God willed to convict of unthankfulness all those who today do not humble themselves to honor his Only Son, when he sent such a multitude of angels to declare that he was the Redeemer who had been promised. It is foolish, then, for us to be satisfied in our unbelief, as we see many stupid people are who do not take account of everything that is contained in the Gospel. There are even mockers of God, who are so careless that it makes no difference what is preached to them. They pay no more attention than they would to fables.

In St. Luke's narration, there is also something which convicts all those who do not subject themselves to honor our Lord Jesus Christ, something which convicts them of a stubborn and devilish rebellion. For since there are unbelievers, they will have an infinite multitude of angels from Paradise who will testify against them. For these are the ministers of the truth of God. Therefore, even though all the wicked and all those who are steeped in their vices and corruptions take pleasure in their sin and are hardened as much as they wish in their unbelief, they have more than sufficient witnesses to testify to their condemnation. For the angels of Paradise appeared so that there might no longer be any excuse for us not to receive Jesus Christ as our sovereign King, humbly bowing ourselves before his majesty.

However, let us note on the other hand that God brought about our salvation when he sent such a multitude of angels, so that we might be able to come to our Lord Jesus Christ with a unresisting courage and that we might no longer be held back by arguments or misgivings but that we might be completely determined that we will find in him all that is lacking in us and that he will have something to provide for all our needs and miseries. Briefly, it is he through whom God willed to communicate himself to us. Do we wish to seek our life anywhere else except in God?

There is complete fullness of the Godhead in Jesus Christ. Therefore, when we have such a testimony, it is just as if God extended his two arms to make us feel his immeasurable goodness. Such a testimony also shows that only when we have a faith in Jesus Christ (I mean a faith without hypocrisy) which leans only on him, knowing that we must receive everything from him, then we will share in all the benefits which we lack and for which we starve. Besides, although today we do not see the angels who appeared only for an instant, yet this testimony is recorded so as to be convincing. For the Holy Spirit spoke through the mouth of St. Luke. Let us be satisfied, then, to have such a witness from God, who declares to us that the angels testified about the birth of our Lord Jesus Christ, so that, knowing how he was made man, that is, that he emptied himself for our sakes, we may be so delighted that we seek the Kingdom of heaven in order to cling to him in true union of faith.

## BETHLEHEM

Next we consider the place of his birth, Bethlehem. This is no small or unimportant testimony when we see how the Son of God was born, just as a long time before, the prophet mentioned it. If the home of Joseph and Mary had been in Bethlehem and if they had made their residence there, it might not have been strange that she delivered there and that Jesus Christ was born there. But this testimony which ought to help us today has often been hidden. For one might at least know that not without reason the prophet had said, "You, Bethlehem, although you are despised as a little village today, yet you will produce him who will be head of my people." But when Joseph and Mary are living in Nazareth and they come into the city of Bethlehem just when she must deliver and Jesus Christ is born there, who will not see that God guided the whole thing by his hand? People, then, must knowingly and with some mischief be blind when they are not willing to recognize the Word of God, which marked his only Son, so he could be received without any doubt as the one who had been promised.

The decree published by the Roman Emperor was certainly sufficient reason to cause Joseph to come to Bethlehem. But bringing a pregnant woman there who was about to deliver was certainly not directed by a human being. God was at work there. We see how God even uses strange means to accomplish his will. For the decree of Caesar, though it was carried out without tyrannical subjection, made it necessary that the Jewish people were then tagged. The Romans had a check upon each person, and it was to show the Jewish people that they did not need to expect any liberty. Jesus Christ was promised to deliver the Jews and all believers from the subjection of Satan and from all tyranny. It seemed that this decree was to close the door, that God might never accomplish what he had promised to his people. However, the decree is the means of accomplishing it. For when Joseph and Mary come as poor people subject to a tyrant, a pagan and an unbeliever, with the result that Jesus Christ is born in Bethlehem, it shows the prophecy to be true. God (as I have said) gives complete certainty here to his own people so that they must not doubt the birth of our Lord Jesus Christ. This, then, is how we must apply the things discussed here to our own use and instruction. For it is not the intention of St. Luke, or rather of the Holy Spirit who spoke by his mouth, simply to write us a history of what had happened. But he expressed here on the one hand how the Son of God did not spare himself for our sakes, and then on the other hand how he provided infallible testimony that he was the Redeemer in order that he might be received as such.

## THE SONG OF THE ANGELS

Let us remember to benefit from this history, so that we may be able to be in tune with the song of the angels in glorifying God, and to receive what he gives us here in such a way that our souls rejoice. In the first place the angel (that is the one who brings the message to the shepherds) says, "Do not be afraid. I announce to you a great joy." (cf. Luke 2:10) Then there is this communal testimony from all the army that God sends, "Peace on earth to men." (cf. Luke 2:14) This, then, is what we must remember first of all: that we seek our joy in Jesus Christ. For, in fact, even if we had all kinds of delights and luxuries, it would only be a matter of drowning ourselves in our pleasures. Even if we are numbed by too many pleasures, even entirely stupid, our conscience will never have repose. We will be endlessly and unceasingly tormented. This worm (of which the Scripture speaks) will eat us away, we will be condemned by our sins, and we will feel that God is perfectly right in being our enemy and opposed to us. So, there will be a curse on all the pleasures of the world, since they will be changed into gnashing of teeth, until people are right with God.

Cursed then are all pleasures, all honors, all things desirable, until we feel that God has received us in mercy. Being thus reconciled with him we can enjoy ourselves, not merely with an earthly joy, but especially with that joy which is promised to us in the Holy Spirit, in order that we may seek it in him. For peace and joy are inseparable things. For how, seeing we are surrounded by so many miseries, can we enjoy ourselves? Moreover, since we are cursed in Adam, we are children of wrath and God is our Judge and is armed with vengeance in order to throw us into the pit. When we are in such a condition, what joy can we imagine? Certainly when we think of it, not only must we be overwhelmed with anxiety but in a horrible hell which is worse than all the sufferings of this world, unless the devil has bewitched us as he seems to have done to many we see who do not stop making merry even though they are making war on God. But if we have a single bit of feeling in us, we will certainly be in torment until God is declared favorable toward us.

It is necessary, therefore, that this peace comes first, namely, that we know that God owns us as his children, especially since he does not impute to us our sins. Are we thus at peace with God? Then we really have something about which to rejoice, even with God, given what I have already said. For unbelievers indeed have some peace (that is to say, they are so dull that they are not concerned about the judgment of God; they even defy it), but it is not peace with God. For they never have peace nor repose, except when they forget both God and themselves and they are completely unconscious. But St. Paul exhorts us to have peace with God, that is, to look to him, and seek as much as we can to be at peace. In other words, when we draw near him, we are certain and

*Even though this is true, we produce nothing new. We only recite the preaching which was done by the angels of Paradise, and not in a small number but an infinite multitude and a great army.*

assured of his love. How will this be? By the forgiveness of our sins, by the free unmerited love which he has for us in our Lord Jesus Christ.

Let us note well, then, that the peace which the angels of Paradise preach here carried with it this joy, which the first angel had mentioned, saying, "I announce to you a great joy," that is, the salvation you will have in Jesus Christ. He is called our Peace, and this title declares that we would be entirely alienated from God unless he received us by means of his only Son. Consequently we also have something to boast of when God accepts us as his children, when he gives us freedom to claim him openly as our Father, to come freely to him, and to have our refuge in him.

However, let us conclude from this that God has arranged that the Gospel be preached by the mouth of humans even though the angels preached it previously. Today the church must be taught by means of mortal creatures. Even though this is true, we produce nothing new. We only recite the preaching which was done by the angels of Paradise, and not in a small number but an infinite multitude and a great army. Besides, we will never be as inflamed to glorify our God as when we are made fully certain of his goodness. That is why these two things are joined: that the angels exhort the entire world to glorify God, since he has given such a peace on earth. We rejoice, then, over the good that God has freed us by means of our Lord Jesus Christ his only Son. He has taken possession of this peace, in order that praises may ascend on high and pierce the clouds and that all the world may re-echo this song, that is, that God may be blessed and glorified everywhere.

We have to conclude from this that we will always be speechless and that we will never be able to praise God until he has made us experience his goodness. For example, how will poor sinners, while they have troubles and regret for their sins and do not know whether God loves them or hates them, be able to bless his name? The anguish, as it were, will keep them restrained so that they will not be able in any way to open their mouths. It must be, therefore, that God first knowingly testifies to us the love he has for us, and does this in such a way that we are determined that he will always be Father to us. Then we will certainly have something for which to bless his name.

133

But since we cannot praise God until he has declared his goodness to us, let us also learn not to have a dead or idle faith, but to be roused to bless the name of God when we see that he has displayed the great treasures of his mercy toward us. May our mouth, on the one hand, perform its function, and then may all our life correspond to it. For this is the true song, that each person dedicates oneself to the service of God, knowing that, since he has bought us at such a price, it is reasonable that all our thoughts and our works be applied to this use, namely, that his name be blessed.

When we know that we really are his own, may we know that it is because it has pleased him to accept us and that everything proceeds from his free generosity. So not without reason is the word added that peace is given to men—not for any merit, not that they had acquired it, but by the good pleasure of God. For the word which St. Luke uses means that we must not seek any other reason why our Lord Jesus Christ appeared to us than that God has had pity and compassion on our miseries. As John 3:16 also says, God so loved the world that he did not spare his own Son, but delivered him to death for our sakes.

## THE LORD'S SUPPER

Let us learn, then, to come to our Lord Jesus Christ in this way: may the message which is published here by the angels be as a burning lamp to us, in order to show us the way that faith leads us and so that we may know that he is now God in us as much as he is God with us. Our God with us is declared when he willed to dwell in our human nature as in his temple. But now he is God in us, that is, we feel him joined to us in greater power than when he showed and declared himself a mortal man. He is even both God and man in us. For first by the power of his Holy Spirit he makes us alive. Then he is man in us, since he makes us share in the sacrifice which he offered for our salvation, and tells us that for good reason he declared that his flesh was truly meat and his blood was truly drink.

This is also why the holy table is made ready for us, so that we may know that our Lord Jesus, after descending here below and emptying himself of everything, was not separated from us when he ascended into his glory in heaven. But rather it is on this condition that we share in his body and his blood. And why? Because we know that his righteousness and obedience are the satisfaction for our sins and that he appeased the wrath of God by the sacrifice of his body and of his blood which he offered in this humanity which he took from us.

Therefore, may we not doubt when Jesus Christ invites us to this table that, although we perceive only bread and wine, he really dwells in us, and may we not doubt that we are so joined to him that there is nothing of himself that

*Therefore, may we not doubt when Jesus Christ invites us to this table that, although we perceive only bread and wine, he really dwells in us, and may we not doubt that we are so joined to him that there is nothing of himself that he is not willing to communicate to us.*

he is not willing to communicate to us. May we recognize these things, I say, so that we know how to profit from this sacrament which he has established for us. However and whenever we receive it, may we know with assurance that God might have delivered us from the depth of condemnation in which we were in another way if he had so willed. But he willed to give us more assurance of the love which he has for us by giving us Jesus Christ as a Guarantee, so that we seek all our good in him. May we know that we cannot fully appreciate what this is, until he is given, as it were, in our midst and is approached by us so that through him we are led into the Kingdom of heaven, from which we were banished and deprived because of our sins.

This is how our Lord Jesus Christ must be applied to our salvation, if we wish to approach God, if we desire to have a real spiritual joy, contentment, and repose, and if we desire to be armed against the temptations which the devil can stir up. But in order to share in this holy table, let us examine ourselves, and let us in the first place recognize our miseries, so that we are offended and completely distressed by them. Then let us also know that God willed to sweeten all our sadness and anguish when he poured himself out in his only Son, and that he willed that we should enjoy him fully.

Although we experience much poverty in this world and are harassed by enemies who are like ravenous wolves, although the devil never stops seeking to devour us and unbelievers bark like powerful dogs, although, I say, we are disturbed by many troubles and endangered from all sides, although we must endure many annoyances, let us hold as beyond doubt that we will always have peace with our God. Let us pray to him that he will make us experience it by his Holy Spirit, since that is one thing that surpasses all human understanding (as we have already noticed from St. Paul). And let us also learn to be so content with our Lord Jesus Christ and the spiritual benefits of which he makes us share, that we may be able to endure patiently all the miseries and afflictions of this world.

It will not turn out to be evil for us to be disturbed from all sides, in brief, to be exposed to all shames and disgrace, provided that Jesus Christ is with us and blesses all our miseries and afflictions. And may we gain such benefit from it that we realize in the middle of all our poverty that we ask nothing except to glorify our God. And when worldly people are successful and thus distressed, since they cannot enjoy themselves without fighting against God, may our true joy be to serve him with complete fear and humility and to give ourselves fully to obeying him. That is how we must benefit from this doctrine.

Now let us bow in humble reverence before the majesty of our God.

# I GREET
# MY SURE REDEEMER

A text from sixteenth-century Strasbourg, first printed along with several metrical settings of the biblical Psalms by Clément Marot, and long associated with the work of John Calvin. This English text is based on a translation by Elizabeth L. Smith (1868).

*I greet my sure Redeemer and my King.*
*You are my trust; accept the love I bring.*
*What pain you suffered, Jesus, for my sake;*
*I pray you from our hearts all cares to take.*

*You are the King of mercy and of grace,*
*Reigning omnipotent in every place;*
*So come, O King, and our whole being sway;*
*Shine on us with the light of your pure day.*

*You are the life by which alone we live*
*And all our substance and our strength receive.*
*Sustain us by your faith and by your power,*
*And give us strength in every trying hour.*

*You have the true and perfect gentleness.*
*You have no harshness and no bitterness.*
*Lord, grant to us the grace in you we see*
*That we may live in perfect unity.*

*Our hope is founded on your holy Word.*
*Our faith is built on every promise, Lord.*
*Grant us your peace; make us so strong and pure*
*That we may conquerors be, all ills endure.*

# Source Information
# and Bibliography

The texts printed here are adapted from previously published English translations, wherever possible in light of original language editions, with a view toward accessibility for modern readers, roughly corresponding with a dynamic equivalance approach to Bible translation. Headings and paragraph breaks within the sermons are added by editors. Each sermon text has its own complicated history. Some texts were taken down by stenographers, some are from editions based on the preacher's own notes or manuscripts. Some of these texts were carefully edited by the preacher or a later editor; others not.

Each hymn text has been not only translated, but also edited by subsequent hymnal editors. Most of the hymn texts presented here are drawn from versions presented in recently published hymnals. Our (difficult) decision to use more recent versions of the hymn texts allows for readers to identify with their own experience of singing these texts and even to hum a line or two as they work through this book. These texts often reflect adaptations of the original, mostly nineteenth-century translations; some of the adaptations actually improve the accuracy of the translations of the original text.

While we think that the texts presented here are useful for devotional use, we also wish to stress that academic studies of these texts should be based on the original sources and editions for texts provided here, with awareness of the multiple translations available for each.

"O Gladsome Light." See the Greek "Phos Hilaron," in John A. McGuckin, *At the Lighting of the Lamps: Hymns of the Ancient Church* (Harrisburg: Morehouse, 1995), 18.

Sermon 1. Jerome, "On the Nativity of Christ, Homily 88," in *The Homilies of Saint Jerome*, ed. Marie Liguori Ewald, in *The Fathers of the Church*, vol. 57 (Washington, DC: Catholic University of America Press, 1966), 221–28. Used by permission. For the Latin text, see *S. Hieronymni presbyteri opera, pars II, opera homiletica*, ed. Gérard Morin, *Corpus Christianorum Series Latina*, vol. 78 (Turnholt, Belgium: Brepols, 1958), 524–29.

"Savior of the Nations, Come." For the Latin "Veni, Redemptor Gentium," see Phillip Wackernagel, *Das deutsche Kirchenlied von der altesten zeit bis zu Anfang des 17. Jahrhunderts*, vol. 1 (Hildesheim, Germany: G. Olms, 1964), 16–17. English translation by Calvin Seerveld, © 1987. Used by permission.

Sermon 2. Augustine, "Sermon 184, On the Birthday of Our Lord Jesus Christ," in *St. Augustine: Sermons on the Liturgical Season*, trans. Mary Sarah Muldowney, R.S.M., in *The Fathers of the Church*, vol. 38 (Washington, DC: Catholic University of America Press, 1959), 3–6. Used by permission. Other versions appear in "On Christmas Day," in *The Works of Saint Augustine: A Translation for the 21st Century*, trans. Edmund Hill (New Rochelle, NY: New City Press, 1993), pt. 3, vol. 6, 17–20, and William Griffin, *Augustine of Hippo: Sermons to the People* (New York: Image Books, 2002), 55–60. The Latin text can be found in D. C. Lambot, O.S.B., *Sancti Aurelii Augustini Hipponensis Episcopi. Sermones selecti duodeviginti*, in *Stromata patristica et mediaevalia* (Brussels, 1950), Sermon 184, 74–76.

"Let All Mortal Flesh Keep Silence." For the Greek text, see *Historical Companion to Hymns Ancient and Modern* (London: William Clowes, 1962), 346. The translation, with slight alterations, is printed in several modern hymnals.

Sermon 3. Leo, "Sermon 21," in *Leo the Great: Sermons*, trans. Jane Patricia Freeland, C.S.J.B. and Agnes Josephine Conway, S.S.J., in *The Fathers of the Catholic Church*, vol. 93 (Washington, DC: Catholic University of America Press, 1996), 77–79. Used by permission. The Latin text can be found in *Sancti Leonis Magni Romani Pontificis: Tractatus Septem et Nonaginta*, ed. Antonius Chavasse, *Corpus Christianorum Series Latina*, vol. 138 (Turnholt, Belgium: Brepols, 1973), 85–89.

"Of the Father's Love Begotten." See Latin "Corde natus ex Parentis," in *Historical Companion to Hymns Ancient and Modern* (London: William Clowes, 1962), 443–44.

Sermon 4. Caesarius of Arles, "On the Birth of Christ the Lord," in *Saint Caesarius of Arles: Sermons*, vol. 3, trans. Mary Magdeleine Mueller, in *The Fathers of the Church*, vol. 66 (Washington, DC: Catholic University of America Press, 1973), 21–24. Used by permission. The Latin text can be found in *Caesarii Arelatensis opera*, ed. G. Morin, *Corpus Christianorum Series Latina*, vol. 103 (Turnholt, Belgium: Brepols, 1953), 775–77.

"Hark! A Thrilling Voice Is Sounding." See Latin "Vox clara ecce intonate," in *Historical Companion to Hymns Ancient and Modern* (London: William Clowes, 1962), 153.

Sermon 5. Gregory the Great, "Homily 8," *Forty Gospel Homilies*, trans. Dom David Hurst (Kalamazoo, MI: Cistercian Publications, 1990), 54–61. Adapted from the translation of David Hurst OSB, *Gregory the Great: Forty Gospel Homilies* (Kalamazoo, MI: Cistercian Publications, 1990). Used with permission. For the Latin text, see J. P. Migne, *Patrologia Latina Series Completa*, vol. 76 (Paris, 1884), 1110C–1114B.

"O Splendor of God's Glory Bright." See Latin text "Splendor paternae gloriae," in John A. McGuckin, *At the Lighting of the Lamps: Hymns of the Ancient Church* (Harrisburg: Morehouse, 1995), 36.

Sermon 6. Bede, *Homilies on the Gospels*, trans. Lawrence T. Martin and David Hurst (Kalamazoo, MI: Cistercian Publications, 1991), 44–51. Adapted from the translation of Lawrence T. Martin and David Hurst OSB, *Homilies on the Gospel* (Kalamazoo, MI: Cistercian Publications, 1991). Used with permission. For the Latin text, see Bede, the Venerable, *The Miscellaneous Works of Venerable Bede, in the original Latin, collated with the manuscripts, and various printed editions, accompanied by a new English translation of the historical works, and a life of the author*, ed. J. A. Giles, vol. 5 (London: Whittaker, 1843), 382.

"Creator of the Stars of Night." See Latin "Conditor alme siderum," in *Historical Companion to Hymns Ancient and Modern* (London: William Clowes, 1962), 152.

Sermon 7. Rabanus Maurus of Mainz, "Sermon before our Lord's Nativity." Adapted from George McCracken and Allen Cabaniss, trans. and eds., *Early Medieval Theology. Library of Christian Classics, volume 9* (Philadelphia: Westminster Press, 1957), 302–4. *Early Medieval Theology (Library of Christian Classics)*, altered. Used by permission of Westminster John Knox Press. For Latin text, see J. P. Migne, *Patrologia Latina Series Completa*, vol. 110 (Paris, 1884), col. 1101B–0012A.

"A Great and Mighty Wonder." See Greek text in *Historical Companion to Hymns Ancient and Modern* (London: William Clowes, 1962), 169.

Sermon 8. Guerric of Igny, "Sermon 10," in Monks of Saint Bernard Abbey, eds. *Guerric of Igny: Liturgical Sermons I*, Cistercian Fathers Series, no. 8 (Shannon, Ireland: Irish University Press, 1971), 61–67. Adapted from the translation of Monks of Saint Bernard Abbey, *Guerric of Igny: Liturgical Sermons I*, (Kalamazoo, MI: Cistercian Publications, 1970). All rights reserved. Used by permission. For the Latin text, see J. P. Migne, *Patrologia Latina Series Completa,* vol. 185 (Paris, 1884), col. 0043B–0046D.

"O Come, O Come Immanuel." See Latin "Veni, veni Immanuel," in *Historical Companion to Hymns Ancient and Modern* (London: William Clowes, 1962), 154–55.

Sermon 9. Bernard of Clairvaux, *The Nativity*, trans. Leo Hickey (Dublin: Scepter Limited, 1959), 1–7. Used by permission. For the Latin text, see J. P. Migne, *Patrologia Latina Series Completa,* vol. 183 (Paris, 1884), 0087A–0090B.

"Jesus, the Very Thought of You." See Latin "Jesu, Dulcis Memoria," in *Historical Companion to Hymns Ancient and Modern* (London: William Clowes, 1962), 249–50.

Sermon 10. John Wyclif, "On the Nativity of Christ," in eds. Clyde E. Fant Jr. and William M. Pinson Jr., *20 Centuries of Great Preaching: An Encyclopedia of Preaching. Vol. 1: Biblical Sermons to Savonarola A.D. 27–1498* (Waco, TX: Word, 1971), 246–47. Adapted by permission. *20 Centuries of Great Preaching, Volume One, Biblical Sermons to Savonarola*, edited by Clyde E. Fant Jr. and William M. Pinson Jr. 1971, W. Publishing (Word, Incorporated), Nashville, Tennessee. All rights reserved.

"Come and Stand Amazed." As published in Psalter Hymnal (Grand Rapids: CRC Publications, 1987) © 1987 CRC Publications, Grand Rapids, MI, 1-800-338-8300. Used by permission.

"O Love How Deep, How Broad, How High." See Latin "O amor quam ecstaticus," in *Historical Companion to Hymns Ancient and Modern* (London: William Clowes, 1962), 248.

Sermon 11. Thomas à Kempis, "On Christmas Night: Of Seeking the Infant Jesus," in *Meditations and Sermons on the Incarnation, Life, and Passion of our Lord, The Works of Thomas à Kempis*, vol. 3, trans. Dom Vincent Scully, C.R.I. (London: Kegan Paul, Trench, Trübner & Co. Ltd., 1907), 83–87. Used by permission.

"In Dulci Jubilo." As translated by S. P. in Percy Dearmer, R. Vaughan Williams, and Martin Shaw, eds. *The Oxford Book of Carols* (Oxford: Oxford University Press, 1928). Translated by Percy Dearmer (1867–1936) © Oxford University Press 1928 from *The Oxford Book of Carols*. Reproduced by permission. For both the Latin/English and Latin/German text, see ibid., 186–88.

Sermon 12. Martin Luther, "Sermon on the Afternoon of Christmas Day 1530," in *Luther's Works*, vol. 51, "Sermons I," trans. and ed. John W. Doberstein (Philadelphia: Muhlenberg Press, 1959), 211–18; WA 32, 261–70. We have omitted the first paragraph of the text in which Luther recounts the sermon he had preached earlier on the same day. From *Luther's Works*, Volume 51 edited by John W. Doberstein, copyright © 1959 Fortress Press. Some language has been modified with permission from the publisher. Used by permission of Augsburg Fortress.

"From Heaven Above." As translated in Roland Bainton, *Martin Luther's Christmas Book* (Minneapolis: Augsburg, 1997), 71–72. Reproduced *Martin Luther's Christmas Book* edited by Roland H. Bainton. Used by permission of Westminster John Knox Press. See also *Luther's Works*, vol. 53, ed. U. S. Leupold (Philadephia: Fortress Press, 1953), 289–91.

Sermon 13. John Calvin, *The Deity of Christ and Other Sermons*, trans. Leroy Nixon (Grand Rapids: Eerdmans, 1950), 35–50. John Calvin, *The Deity of Christ and Other Sermons*, trans. Leroy Nixon, © 1950 Wm. B. Eerdmans Publishing Co., Grand Rapids, MI. Used by permission of the publisher. French text is found in *Ioannis Calvini Opera quae supersunt omnia*, ed. Wilhelm Baum, Edward Cunitz, and Edward Reuss, vol. 46 (Brunsvigae, Switzerland: A. Swetschke and Son, 1891), 955–68.

"I Greet My Sure Redeemer." See the French "Je te salue, mon certain Redempteur," in *Ioannis Calvini Opera quae supersunt omnia*, ed. Wilhelm Baum, Edward Cunitz, and Edward Reuss, vol. 6 (Brunsvigae, Switzerland: A. Swetschke and Son, 1867), 223–24.

John D. Witvliet (Ph.D., University of Notre Dame), is director of the Calvin Institute of Christian Worship and holds faculty appointments in worship, theology, and music at both Calvin College and Calvin Theological Seminary in Grand Rapids, Michigan. He is the author of *Worship Seeking Understanding* (Baker Academic) and coeditor of *Worship in Medieval and Early Modern Europe* (University of Notre Dame Press).

David Vroege is the pastor of All Nations Christian Reformed Church in Halifax, Nova Scotia.